"Like most Christians, I live in a state of denial about the Trinity. Since I cannot explain it, I do not think about it very much. After reading this book, I cannot *stop* thinking about it. Where did belief in the Trinity come from? Why has it been such a contentious article of faith? How does it affect Christians in their relationship with those of other faiths? Why is the Holy Spirit so hard to institutionalize and why is that such good news? Tickle and Sweeney know why all of these questions matter. They furthermore know how to write about them so that they matter to us too. If you want to know more about what is happening to Christian faith and why—and if you are also wiling to discover what it means to love God with your whole *mind*—this is the book for you."

—**Barbara Brown Taylor**, author of *Learning to Walk in the Dark*

"Phyllis Tickle—this time ably assisted by Jon M. Sweeney—continues to document the emergence of a new church, and always with a keen eye to what's gone before. Attentiveness to the Holy Spirit, which this book has in spades, will surely be a hallmark of the next epoch of Christianity. Herein, the ancient and the postmodern walk down the aisle, wedded once and for all."

—**Tony Jones**, theologian-in-residence at Solomon's Porch and editor of *Phyllis Tickle: Evangelist of the Future*, tonyj.net

"If we were all students, and Phyllis Tickle and Jon Sweeney were our history teachers, we'd all be passionate about understanding our past. If they were our theology teachers, we'd all be fascinated to more deeply contemplate the Trinity in the present. And if they were our spiritual directors, we'd be turning our hearts, day by day, to being more guided and empowered by the Spirit to move joyfully into the future. Here is a book that instructs and delights, so this bright possibility can become a reality."

—**Brian D. McLaren**, author/speaker/activist, brianmclaren.net

"When two scholars as eminent as Phyllis Tickle and Jon Sweeney team up to write a book about the most dangerous leg of the Trinity, the Holy Spirit, I would offer a simple but sincere directive: take and read. You will understand why the Great Emergence is indeed upon us, and why God the Spirit is again brooding over the face of the muddy waters of a church that has forgotten where it came from, where it is going, and to Whom it belongs."

—**Rev. Dr. Robin R. Meyers**, senior minister of Mayflower Congregational UCC, Oklahoma City; Distinguished Professor of Social Justice at Oklahoma City University; and author of *The Underground Church: Reclaiming the Subversive Way of Jesus*

"To read Phyllis Tickle is to engage thoughtfully with the fundamental question of religion: what is God and how can a mere human recognize God's presence within the world's noisy clamor? This book is simultaneously rich in scholarship and personally accessible as it explores the nature of spirit with an eye to the enormous challenges of our time. I found it both thought-provoking and moving."

—**T. M. Luhrmann**, author of *When God Talks Back*

The Age
of the Spirit

The Age of the Spirit

How the Ghost *of an* Ancient Controversy Is Shaping the Church

Phyllis Tickle

with JON M. SWEENEY

BakerBooks

a division of Baker Publishing Group
Grand Rapids, Michigan

© 2014 by Phyllis Tickle and Jon M. Sweeney

Published by Baker Books
a division of Baker Publishing Group
P.O. Box 6287, Grand Rapids, MI 49516-6287
www.bakerbooks.com

Printed in the United States of America

Library of Congress Cataloging-in-Publication Data

Tickle, Phyllis.
    The age of the spirit : how the ghost of an ancient controversy is shaping the church / Phyllis Tickle, with Jon M. Sweeney.
        pages cm
    ISBN 978-0-8010-1480-2 (cloth)
    1. Holy Spirit—History of doctrines. I. Title.
BT119.T53 2014
231'.3—dc23   2013022770

14   15   16   17   18   19   20   7   6   5   4   3   2   1

Contents

Contents

The Back Story

The story you are about to read has a back story. That's certainly not unusual. Almost every tale, whether good or bad, has a story behind the story. It's just that some of those stories are more interesting than others. This particular one of ours, however, happens to be not only interesting but also pertinent. It is so very pertinent, in fact, that we must begin by telling it before we get on with the business of telling our central story of the Spirit and this age in which we live.

The story behind our intended story is hardly an unknown one, despite its being labeled as "back." That is, most people in Western or westernized cultures are, to some greater or lesser extent, aware that we who live in the twenty-first century are passing through unusual times—that, indeed, we are passing through almost unprecedented times of change and shift, upheaval and reconfiguration. But while our particular shifts and upheavals may indeed be particular, many of us also know that the timing of their arrival and the generally chaotic nature of their presence are not. Rather, the very appearance of such an era as ours is, historically speaking, right on time.

About every half millennium, give or take a decade or two, the latinized cultures of the world go through a century of enormous upheaval that affects every part of their existence: from economics to politics, from intellectual life to social structures, from cultural norms to religious perceptions. That is to say that those parts of the world that received their Christianity through the Latin language, were colonized by those who so received, or who were colonialized by those who so received are subject to semi-millennial uproars that shift and toss every part of themselves so violently as to reconfigure the whole into new—sometimes almost unrecognizably new—ways of being and thinking.[1]

Five hundred years ago, the peoples and cultures of the latinized world slugged their way through the horrors and glories of the *Great Reformation*. As a time of enormous and precipitous change, the Great Reformation gave the world, among other things, the cultural and intellectual reconfigurations of humanism, the political consequences of a new construct now known as the nation-state, the disorienting and very consequential new social structure of a middle class in a culture where no such thing had ever previously been before, and the economic tsunami of a new way of doing business called capitalism, etc. In the course of all of that, and because religion never floats free of the culture in which it exists and which it informs, the Great Reformation also gave the latinized world that thing we now know as Protestantism or Protestant Christianity.

Similarly, one can look back a thousand years from our twenty-first century and discover, with no effort at all, the *Great Schism* of the eleventh century, with its devastating severance of East from West and of Eastern ways from Western ones in every part of life, including the eviction of Orthodox Christianity from the Western experience and the establishment of Roman Catholicism up out of what had, for half a millennium, been monastic and/or episcopal and/or Mediterranean Christianity.

Fifteen hundred years ago, one finds in the sixth century the horrendous time of heartbreak and upheaval we now refer to as the *Great Decline and Fall*, when all that had been—all that had given ordered governance and economic shape and social cohesion to the classical world—crumbled away, leaving nothing save chaos in its wake. The Dark Ages would stand ever thereafter as Mediterranean and European humanity's most hideous of times; but monastic and conciliar Christianity would rise up out of the ashes of what had been, as would decentralized socio-political units and the impact upon the West of Arabic intellectualism and science.

Two thousand years ago, the shifting and turning were so monumental and so consequential that the dating of time itself has been marked and recorded in terms of it ever since. Despite the fact that, for the sake of political correctness, our choice of wording has gone from "before Christ" (BC) and "anno Domini" (AD) to "before the Common Era" (BCE) and "of the Common Era" (CE), the world still pays homage to the Great Transformation every time a date is noted or a document recorded.

The world fell apart during the years of the *Great Transformation*.[2] Rome moved from being a kingdom to being an empire, and the known world moved from being a composition of disconnected geopolitical entities to being member-parts of a cultural and economic and political whole. Highways connected disparate citizenries physically, and a common monetary system connected them economically. Relatively easy travel and fairly adequate public safety ended up creating unprecedented cultural exchange and cross-insemination of ideas, information, and opinions. The old world was dead and the old ways with it. Empire—worldwide empire—made all things new (and by the way, it also made possible the spread of a variant of

Judaism that would come to be known as Christianity, a variant that would inform and reflect, from its earliest, most formative days, the new mind-set and worldview of the Great Transformation itself).

While chaos and the resulting reconfiguration of every part of life are the hallmarks and informing characteristics of the latinized world's five-hundred-year cycles, there are two other things that must also be said about them just here. The first of these we have known for a long time. The second we have come to grasp only recently, and our recent grasping of it has to do with its suspected relevance to us right here and right now.

We have just begun to admit, in other words, what we should have known and admitted all along: namely, that not all the *Greats* of our cycling history were created equal. One of them—the Great Transformation—has far exceeded the others in impact. We have sensed this historically, but now we are beginning to consider it openly because we are beginning openly to suspect that this thing we call the *Great Emergence* is going to prove itself equal in its impact to that of the Great Transformation. As a thought, such is a fairly unsettling one. But more on that later. It is the other hallmark of the *Greats* that must first command our full attention.

From the Great Transformation to the Great Emergence, every five-hundred-year pivot in latinized history has been marked by (or perhaps one should say haunted by) one overarching question, and that is the question of "Where now is our authority?" Or put another way, as often happens, "How now shall we live?"

What gets lost in the disestablishment of all that has been and the reconfiguration of all that is into some kind of coherent new level of complexity is any clear sense of who is calling the plays, who is making the rules, who is determining the good and contending against the evil. Indeed, the psychic stress of latinized history's semi-millennial upheavals has to do, in large part, with this displacement or loss of norms or rules or working principles. And whether one likes it or not—whether one is a theist or not or whether, in fact, one is a completely secularized miscreant or not—it is still "religion" whose social function it is to answer those questions and articulate for a culture those moral norms and moral imperatives by which life is to be judged and controlled in this new context and emerging circumstance.

For religion and the religious, of course, arriving at the answer to "Where now is our authority?" is not so simple a thing as just constructing a new moral code or revamping an old one to accommodate new times. True, at a practical or political and purely cultural level, religion's discoveries and reformulations may indeed present as little more than a formulary of prescribed values and modes of behavior, but not so for the faithful. For the faithful, the devout, the believer, the pastor or the parishioner, the theolog or the insouciant, the mystic or the rationalist—for all of them, any answer to that fundamental question of authority at any time in history must rest firmly upon something that is religiously credible, something that God has directly sanctioned. For the religious, both now and historically speaking, authority must find its first principles and validation in something that has its foundation firmly planted in the holy writings, in the received tradition, and in the recorded testimony of the elders who have gone before in the faith.

This is all well and good, except for one small problem. When we today, from our place as Christians of the twenty-first century and in the era of the Great Emergence, try to wrestle responsibly with the question of authority for our times and for the centuries that will follow after us, we stumble over the Holy Spirit. Or perhaps better said, we stumble over our inherited confusion about What/Who the Trinity is and, most particularly within that conundrum, about Who/What the Holy Spirit may be. Nowhere, in all our books and treatises and hymns, is there a consistent or coherent record of what the Church before us has understood about these things, and most especially not about the Holy Spirit described within them.

Philosopher and theologian Robin Meyers captures both the conundrum and its causes when he contends that, "The real problem is that the Holy Spirit cannot be controlled by the pen of any theologian."

Of course, in that one brief sentence, Meyers has also caught the uneasy grief in our despair. Declaring that church history itself is largely "subsumed by the tension between mystics and prelates," he goes on to argue quite correctly that in matters of authority, "It is not always fidelity to creeds or doctrines that causes concern. Rather, it is about the appropriate chain of command. Who is really in charge? The word *hierarchy* means 'rule by the holy.' This is why the Holy Spirit is the most dangerous leg of the Trinity, and why the defenders of order make rules and write books."[3]

Harvey Cox, one of our most astute living historians of religion, makes much the same point when he says: "The tensions between ecstasy and order, between spiritual freedom and group cohesion, between mystics and administrators have persisted for the full two thousand years of Christian history. They show no sign of abating."[4] Welcome to our tumultuous times.

And with that unsettling realization, our back story concludes, and our story itself is set free to begin.

Notes

1. The groundwork for much of our tale-telling here, both in the back story and what follows, was laid in *The Great Emergence* in 2008 (Grand Rapids: Baker Books). After *The Great Emergence*, *Emergence Christianity: What It Is, Where It Is Going, and Why It Matters* (Grand Rapids: Baker Books, 2012) described how those who are living within and through the current Emergence reformation moment aim to serve the Kingdom of God in whatever form God is presenting it. *The Age of the Spirit*, a collaboration between Tickle and Sweeney is, then, book number three in a series, as well as being the first in the group to aim itself at illuminating one particular holy hinge upon which the faith of every Christian turns.

2. This is the only one of our *Great* upheavals to have two competing popular names. Some readers, for that reason, may be more familiar with the name the *Great Transition*. Whether transition or transformation matters not. Both refer to the same cataclysmic shift of the first century.

3. Robin R. Meyers, *The Underground Church: Reclaiming the Subversive Way of Jesus* (San Francisco: Jossey-Bass, 2012), 68, 70–71.

4. Harvey Cox, *The Future of Faith* (New York: HarperOne, 2009), 94.

PART 1

Holy Ideas

in UNHOLY CONFLICT

1

Beginning at the Beginning

As a rule, the best way to approach a really loaded question is to commence where the question itself commenced: at the beginning. Sometimes, though, it is even wiser to begin by reminding ourselves of exactly why it is that we are taking on the question in the first place. This is one of those times,

> ... because, whether we like it or not, we live in an era when our fellow citizens tend to be "more spiritual than religious" and yet, despite that surrounding emphasis, we are not quite sure of what the "Spirit" is in mainline and/or historic and/or orthodox Christianity.

> ... because we face renewed charges and/or perhaps an internal concern about whether or not Christianity is truly a monotheistic religion. That concern has never been more important than it is in the present moment. The roots of Islam's early, dramatic growth in the sixth and seventh centuries of the Common Era can be traced, in part, to the furor over the Trinity and all its representations and descriptive presentations. Certainly, in our own time, the charge of polytheism is the one being increasingly

laid at Christianity's doorstep by contemporary Islam. Without a full and rich contemplation of the mystery of the Trinity, we Christians stand defenseless against such summations.

. . . because Pentecostalism is the fastest-growing expression of Christianity, especially in the Southern Hemisphere, where the demographic heft and bulk of global Christianity have now shifted. And whatever else it pivots on, Pentecostal Christianity is poised forever upon the engagement of the Spirit.

. . . because the early Church and our post-apostolic forebears in the faith started life with councils as their ultimate authority. As a result, they—and by extension, we—inevitably ended up with the top-down hierarchies of today, all of which are in some distress and many of which are in extremis. How, then, is religious authority to be determined today? Many—most, in all probability—would say by discernment through the Spirit, which means what?

. . . and because, ready or not, we find ourselves alive and Christian in a time of almost unprecedented upheaval. And this upheaval which we find ourselves in the midst of is apparently going to do nothing less than attempt to discover a fuller and more complete understanding of the Trinity during our lifetime or, barring that, most certainly within the lifetimes of our children and their children.

. . . and because, if that be true, what we are going through right now, which we call the Great Emergence, is indeed more cataclysmic than the Great Reformation or the Great Schism or the Great Decline and Fall ever were. It is right up there with the Great Transformation, when our Lord Himself brought the Christian movement out of Judaism and everything changed, even our way of dating and marking time.

And in view of all of that, what matters is not whether, as individual believers, we are Emergence Christians or traditional Christians.

What matters is that we have arrived at the point in our conversation where we are to begin tracing the strange story of how, as a people of faith, we Christians have envisioned, engaged, and all too often even tried to engineer the Holy Spirit over the millennia. As we do so, however, at least one imperative is upon us. That is, we must remember always—and again, without regard to whether we are Emergence Christians or traditional Christians—to do our story-telling and our discerning with an eye on our own time and with the ears of our souls and of our minds ever and always attuned to the guidance that this story can lend us in this time of our upheaval.

There was, of course, a beginning for this "Holy Spirit and Us" story of ours, and it is recorded, predictably enough, even before we get to the one about Adam and Eve. Within the first two or three dozen words of Scripture, we are told: "In the beginning, God created the heavens and the earth. The earth was without form, and void; and darkness was on the face of the deep. And the Spirit of God was hovering over the face of the waters" (Gen. 1:1–2 NKJV).

The Hebrew word used here for *Spirit* is *ruach*, which means, basically, a disturbance of the air and is, as a result, translated sometimes as *breath*, sometimes as *wind*, sometimes as *Spirit*. As words go, that is, this one, right from the beginning of things, enjoyed not so much a specific definition as it did a connotation of being both the agency and also the proof of the invisible made visible in its consequences. One of the great witticisms or bits of wordplay attributed to Jesus rests, in fact, on His use of this very ambiguity. In telling Nicodemus that unless one is born of water and the Spirit (*pneuma* in Greek), he cannot enter the kingdom of God, Jesus immediately proves His point by citing the wind (again, *pneuma*) as blowing where it wishes, yet none can tell where it comes from or goes to (John 3:5–8).

Ruach itself, with its multifaceted subtleties and teasing nuances, occurs almost four hundred times in Hebrew Scripture. It does everything from inspiring the art of Bezalel, the master craftsman who oversaw the furnishing and decorating of the Tabernacle of Meeting (Exod. 31:2–6), to giving Samson his strength (Judg. 14:6), to bestowing intellectual prowess and understanding (Sir. 39:6), to conveying wisdom and religious knowledge (Wis. 7:7; 9:17). It is also the *ruach*, the prophets say, that will rest upon the Son of David who is to come as Messiah and as Israel's hope (Isa. 11:2; Ezek. 36:26; Joel 2:28; etc.).

The *ruach*, or Spirit, was, in fact, the inspirer of all the great prophets of Judaism right up until the time that prophecy ceased in the land because of the disobedience of the people. There is a rabbinic tradition, however, that holds that Y-H-W-H in His mercy did not entirely withdraw from His people. Instead of speaking to them through the *ruach*, He spoke through the *Bath Qol*: that is, through "the daughter of the Voice of God."

When Messiah comes, that tradition teaches, there will be little or no more need for the *Bath Qol*, for the people will again have direct, and even greater, access to the Spirit. This tradition—this sadness of lost prophesying, this consolation of the daughter of the Voice of God, and this promise that when Messiah came, the Spirit would once more be among us—was well known amongst the disciples and early Jewish Christians. Thus it is that at Jesus's baptism, Mark tells us that the Spirit (*pneuma*) descends on him like a dove *and* that it is the Voice (*phōnē* in Greek), and not the daughter of the Voice, that proclaims him as the well-beloved Son in whom Y-H-W-H finds delight (Mark 1:9–12). It is the Voice, or *phōnē*, and neither the *pneuma* nor the daughter of the Voice, who will appear again at the Transfiguration, where it is the Voice Itself that declares, "This is my beloved Son: hear him" (Mark 9:7 KJV). The power of that distinction and the power of its implication, while usually lost to most Christians today, were certainly not lost on those first disciples and converts.

But with or without the extracanonical tradition of the *Bath Qol* and its suggestive effects, we still must at some point address four things if we are to pursue our story any further. The first of them is easy to accept: Judaism is deeply and wholly monotheistic.[1]

The second thing we must recognize certainly comes out of Judaism's characterizing monotheism, but it is considerably trickier to pin down. That is, as we have seen, Judaism uses a system of multifaceted and suggestive namings when it is speaking of the Spirit that is and is not Y-H-W-H, but is of Him.

The third thing is closely tied to the second but is fairly painless. We must understand, as we begin our story of the Spirit among us, that at least two or three of those Jewish suggestive, rather than definitive, namings came bouncing into Christianity's continuation of the story right from its very beginning.

The fourth thing that impacts our tracing of the Spirit's story is more difficult to resolve. That is, we as Christians can neither think nor speak of the Spirit without thinking or speaking, either directly or by implication, of the Trinity itself. The truth of things, however, is that neither the Hebrew Bible nor our New Testament ever employs—or even mentions—the word *Trinity* as such at all. What that means, at a working level, is that there is no better or more available way into the heart of our adventure than to look at the Spirit's story chronologically. That is, we are best served in our study if we look first at the Spirit as Spirit, and then at Spirit as within a Trinity, and then, finally, at Spirit as one of three distinct and approachable and "personed" Great Truths within a Great Truth.

On, then, to the next stage of our exploration.

Note

1. The very centerpiece and foundation of all Jewish prayer is the *Shema*: "Hear, O Israel: The LORD our God, the LORD is one" (Deut. 6:4 NKJV).

2

An Ancient Conversation in Our Shifting Times

Scripture may not mention the word *Trinity* as such, but it does most certainly speak of God's Holy Spirit, even as it employs a variety of metaphors in doing so. Metaphors, while they may not always be helpful, are sometimes all we have. At times, they can also be more instructive to the heart's understanding than would be other, more overt and reasoned declarations. One suspects—must suspect, in fact—that such is the case here.

In the moments of Transfiguration where the Voice of God spoke, God's Spirit is also present, as we have already noted, and is perceived as a cloud in the sky. Thus, Luke 9:34–35:

> While he was saying this, a cloud came and overshadowed them; and they were terrified as they entered the cloud. Then from the cloud came a voice that said, "This is my Son, my Chosen; listen to him!"[1]

That cloud, like the presence of the Voice, was for early Christian theologians pivotal and very telling. It was understood by them as being the same cloud that guided the Israelites through the wilderness, and the catenation of one story to another—the tying of a contemporary event to the wonder of an inherited one—rejoiced their hearts just as it affirmed them in their new faith.[2]

In much the same way, the word that is used by Luke in his telling of the Transfiguration and that is translated as *overshadowed* in English is the word he also uses in his telling of the Annunciation of the angel Gabriel to the Virgin Mary:

> The angel said to her, "The Holy Spirit will come upon you, and the power of the Most High will overshadow you; therefore the child to be born will be holy; he will be called Son of God." (Luke 1:35)

There are symbols for the Spirit in Scripture, as well as metaphors, of course. Oil is the most prominent of them. The Second Letter to the Corinthians offers us one of the earliest instances of how the oil of Jewish ritual was readily imported into the Christian movement, entering liturgical practice for anointing and consecration:

> But it is God who establishes us with you in Christ and has anointed us, by putting his seal on us and giving us his Spirit in our hearts as a first installment. (2 Cor. 1:21–22)

And then, from the very beginning, there are avatars: ways in which the Holy Spirit in Scripture is said to literally embody other creatures and created things. A dove, a rushing wind, a fire—all of them come readily to mind:

> And when Jesus had been baptized, just as he came up from the water, suddenly the heavens were opened to him and he saw the

Spirit of God descending like a dove and alighting on him. (Matt. 3:16)

And suddenly from heaven there came a sound like the rush of a violent wind, and it filled the entire house where they were sitting. Divided tongues, as of fire, appeared among them, and a tongue rested on each of them. (Acts 2:2–3)

Metaphors, symbols, avatars: they are all difficult, but even more difficult is the fact that neither in them nor anywhere else is the Holy Spirit presented in Holy Writ as a "person" in the sense that a human being may be presented as a "person." As Augustine himself pointed out, nowhere in Scripture is there mention of "three *persons*."[3] Indeed, quite to the contrary, we have Paul's very clear words to the Ephesians:

There is one body and one Spirit . . . one Lord, one faith, one baptism, one God and Father of all, who is above all and through all and in all. (Eph. 4:4–6)

In this, of course, Paul could well have had in mind Jesus's own words of "I and the Father are one" (John 10:30 NIV). Yet Paul wrote his "one body, one Spirit, one Lord" words also fully cognizant of the Great Commission. That is, Paul of all people would have been aware of Jesus's words:

Go therefore and make disciples of all nations, baptizing them in the name of the Father and of the Son and of the Holy Spirit. (Matt. 28:19)

What, then, did Paul or any of those first-century hearers and readers of the Gospel understand by Jesus's words, by those three different apparent names for God? We don't know and, because we don't know, we flounder now as we have floundered for centuries.[4] If we are honest, in other words, then we must admit to ourselves and to everybody else that there is no aspect of creedal Christianity that makes more Christians uneasy today than does the whole area of the existence, reality, and workings of God in the person of the Holy Spirit. Put another way, this central mystery within a central mystery may indeed be central, but it still unnerves us.[5]

To grossly (but perhaps not unfairly) generalize, most liturgical Christians—that is, most of us still connected to communions that existed prior to the Great Reformation—are rather comfortable with God the Father. Most of us who are Protestants, and especially those of us who are evangelicals, are quite comfortable with God the Son. On the other hand, too much public talk about Jesus to those of us who are, for example, Anglicans, may make for a lot of squirming. And anyone who wants to bore an audience of evangelicals into total lassitude only has to talk about God the Father for more than ninety seconds.[6] Thus it goes among us except for one informing fact: if anyone wants to make all of the above equally edgy, then let him or her start talking about the Holy Spirit.

But as everybody knows, Christians have had this discomforting confusion for centuries; so the prior—or perhaps, the primal—question does indeed become one of asking why the whole thing is so disturbing to us now. We have looked already at why, of necessity, we must ask the question in our time, but that is not the same thing at all as trying to ascertain what it is that makes us so uncomfortable about even entering into the exploration in the first place.

The answer to that one is either very simple or incalculably complex, depending on how far one wants to push it. For our purposes, perhaps it is sufficient simply to say first that we suffer a sense of discomforting confusion and urgency because as Christians, many of us are increasingly surrounded by fellow Christians who aren't

"Christian" in the old, traditional, creed-defined way—who, in other words and by their own admission, aren't Christian in the old tried and true ways as those ways have been understood for almost two thousand years, or better put, as we understood them right up until about five or six decades ago.

If history teaches us anything, it most certainly teaches us that times change, and so do eras, the latter category being even more compelling than the former just by virtue of sheer size and magnitude. Ours is a shifting era. The century and a half of the peri-Emergence—those decades that immediately preceded our present time—changed essentially every part of our lives. Among the most seismic of those shifts was the one from a rural to an urban milieu, from a more socially and personally constricted and physically connected lifestyle to one that granted millions of us greater blocks of free time and that most certainly invited greater exploration of the interior life, both one's own and that of others.

In a sense, for those of us in the latinized or Western world, human subjectivity was born in those years—or if not born, then certainly discovered at a mass and popular level. Spurred on by exponentially increased opportunities to engage the non-physical, we began to engage our selves more and more.[7] Subjectivity, however, proved to be a hinterland that institutionalized Christianity could neither accommodate nor serve as reliable tour guide for.[8] As a result (and as a good Buddhist might say), the decades of the peri-Emergence saw the untethering of monkey minds in the vast majority of us.

Thus untethered and unattended, within a matter of little more than a century and a half, millions of us in the latinized world were on our way to new internal or religious adventures—to new ways of being aware, to new ways of engaging wonder and exercising awe and connecting with the power beyond the visible. Many of us were on our way to becoming more deliberately spiritual but not religious.

Many others of us were on our way to becoming Pentecostals or Charismatics. And a very vocal cadre of us were on our way to becoming practitioners of religionless Christianity. But however we may choose to slice and dice the peri-Emergence's urbanizing, modernizing shift and its consequences, the conversation inevitably will always wind back around again to words like "spirit," or "spiritual," or even "Spirit." And all of us—whether we be traditionals or "spiritual but not religious" or Pentecostals or proponents of religionlessness or just ordinary folk—can feel the shifting currents in that wind as it blows around us.[9]

Notes

1. In this regard, the reader may want to look again at page 22.
2. Cf. Exodus 13:21.
3. See Augustine, *Trin.* 7.4.
4. The centuries of floundering have left their own painful and sometimes bloody records. Sometimes all those battles, won and lost only to be fought again years later, also left a paper trail. That is, they also, for better or worse, affected the transmission of Scripture. A case in point is the mistake known to scholars as the Johannine Comma that appears in the King James Bible's version of 1 John 5:7: "For there are three that bear record *in heaven, the Father, the Word, and the Holy Ghost: and these three are one*" (emphasis added).

Simply put, someone added the comma, or clause, that is printed here in italics. The mystery surrounding the copyist's addition is worthy of a mystery thriller in and of itself, so clear is the theological agenda behind it, i.e., with this simple addition to the text of an obscure epistle perhaps we can quell the questioning about our distinctive, central claim to a Godhead in three persons. It would now appear to all concerned that the Trinity is mentioned explicitly in Scripture after all.

The addition to the text arose first in manuscripts of the New Testament in the fourth century and appeared for the first time in English in 1522, due to a faulty manuscript that had likely been glossed or otherwise changed. When Erasmus was translating his Greek New Testament in 1514, he left the clause out, knowing that it was a corruption of the earliest extant texts, but after protests, he put it back in for the publication of his complete Greek Bible in 1522. Hence, it entered the so-called *Textus Receptus*, and thus, the KJV.

Whether the Church of the twenty-first century wishes to do so or not, the time has arrived in which we must grapple with this very central doctrine in a way that frees it from human manipulation and opens it to the telling of the Spirit.

5. Robin Meyers articulates this state of affairs very well indeed when he describes the Holy Spirit as "the most mysterious, the most important, and the most disorienting force in the body of Christ" (Meyers, *The Underground Church: Reclaiming the Subversive Way of Jesus* [San Francisco: Jossey-Bass, 2012], 68). This vagueness or sense of discomfort did not always accrue apparently. If, for example, we read the Letter to the Romans, we find an intimacy with the Spirit that is almost endearing: "Likewise the Spirit helps us in our weakness; for we do not know how to pray as we ought, but that very Spirit intercedes with sighs too deep for words. And God, who searches the heart, knows the mind of the Spirit, because the Spirit intercedes for the saints according to the will of God" (Rom. 8:26–27).

6. This is why Jaroslav Pelikan, the eminent historical theologian and convert from Lutheranism to Eastern Orthodoxy, once remarked in an interview with the editor of *Christianity Today*: "You evangelicals talk too much about Jesus and don't spend enough time thinking about the Holy Trinity." (Quoted in David Neff, "The Fullness and the Center: Bishop Kallistos Ware on Evangelism, Evangelicals, and the Orthodox Church," *Christianity Today*, July 2011, 41.)

7. The history of psychology, and later of psychiatry and neuroscience and psychobiology, etc., is itself a history of this shift. From the early days of Mesmer in the mid-nineteenth century to the probing work in consciousness studies today, the line of evolving exploration and understanding bears testimony to the power and compelling absorption we have had with subjectivity for the last sixteen or seventeen decades. So, for that matter, does the history of philosophy over the last century and a half and/or that of literature.

8. At a somewhat less remarked-upon level, we are surrounded by various and varying institutionalized attempts to reconcile, during the years of the peri-Emergence, these early shifts toward a new emphasis on the Spirit and on the spiritual with historic Christianity's lack of clarity about the Trinity. Everything from Theosophy to New Thought, from the Unitarian Church's assertion of a singular Godhead to the Church of the Latter-day Saints' insistence on three Gods united in one purpose, bears evidence to that struggle, all of them having been born during the peri-Emergence.

9. Statistics about the size of the "spiritual but not religious" among us presently do not separate out Christians from non-Christians within the category. Likewise, there is no numerical count yet of Christians who adhere to a "religion-less Christianity" or "Christianity after religion," as opposed to institutionalized Christianity. There are, however, reliable figures available about the size of the Pentecostal and Charismatic (often lumped together by demographers as Renewalists) population. Those figures consistently show that about one in every four professing Christians on earth falls into this category.

3

The Great Enigma

Perhaps St. Augustine, one of Christianity's earliest and greatest theologians, put the matter in its proper light when, as a young convert and fledgling priest, he began to contend that, "Every measure of Christian progress comes through a spiritual and reasoned understanding of the Trinity."[1]

The difficulty Augustine was wrestling with in the late fourth century would come, in time, to be known as *enigma fidei*, or perhaps better said as the *enigma fidei*: the *"enigma of the faith."* That's what the famous Benedictine-turned-Cistercian abbot William of St. Thierry called the Holy Trinity seven hundred years after St. Augustine's observation, and *enigma fidei* it has remained ever since.

Abbot William wrote a book about the whole thing in the twelfth century, claiming, even as he did so, that the Trinity is an inexplicable mystery. Despite that acknowledgment and following in the way of many other theologians, Abbot William went on—at considerable length, in fact—to try to explain the entire matter anyway.

On the other hand, and to give William his just due, there have never, up until recently, been many Christians, other than professional or academic religionists like him, who have even been equipped to work on, or sustain much interest in, the business of defining the Trinity. The truth of the thing is that until the last century or so, most of us in the naves and pews of Christendom have rarely known enough about the history of the faith to pause for long over theological mysteries. Even more rarely have we ever thought to ask where and how an idea like the Trinity got started. But our times are not like those of our Christian ancestors. Unlike them, we know that we can no longer speak, even cautiously, about God, the Holy Spirit—or for that matter, about God, the Father or God, the Son—without speaking of Being-nesses inherent within an Is-ness that has no Being-nesses.

All of this is not to suggest, of course, that we—whether laity or congregational clergy—have consistently ignored our Trinitarian confusions for the last two thousand years or that we have in any way failed to acknowledge over the centuries since St. Augustine the Trinity's foundational place in Christianity. Quite the opposite has been true, in fact, and as a result, thousands and thousands of our fellow Christians have died over those centuries defending one Trinitarian position or another.[2] It is more accurate, then, to say that over the years since the fourth century CE, many, but hardly all of us, have simply been fairly insouciant about the whole thing. The irony or disconnect in all of our historic nonchalance really does lie, as Augustine says, in the irrefutable fact that the Trinity is a central and defining mystery of Christianity. Without it, we are no more than organized moralists and well-intentioned citizens of our various secular polities.

Some would argue, of course (and probably quite accurately), that it is the very centrality—the so-called horrible wonder—of "Trinity" which has turned us and most of our forebears into infantile believers: that it is the inscrutable terror of offending such mystery that has made us all too willing to be satisfied with and/or deterred by the easy metaphors of workaday sermons and well-intentioned but one-size-must-fit-all Bible studies.[3] Who among us does not remember having been instructed by at least some of those?[4]

Who, for example, does not remember Sunday school tricks with a "holy triangle" on a chalkboard or with a three-leafed clover plucked from the church lawn? Or a shamrock pulled from an old St. Patrick's Day poster? Or what about that somewhat more urbane and sophisticated example of a fleur-de-lis? Or, for that matter, who can forget those brief, distressing moments when from the pulpit an actual pretzel, salt and all, was used to illuminate Christianity's most sacred secret?[5]

There are, of course, less inane but still popular metaphors that attempt to use scientific or quasi-scientific categories to explain this thing that seems inexplicable but that we somehow feel should be "tangible" or "graspable." One of the more ubiquitous of those pseudo-scientific metaphors uses space and its three primary components: height, width, and depth (but conveniently omitting time, of course). Another employs the three forms of H_2O: solid, liquid, and vapor—i.e., ice, water, and steam. But therein lies at least part of the tale, for all of these contrivances of ours, whether recent or less so, are variances on the most common and oldest (we can date it from the third century CE right into the twenty-first) theological error in all of Christianity: modalism.

A modalist is a Christian who, whether intentionally or not, explains the three persons of the Trinity to himself or others as aspects or personalities or "modes" of one God and then, having done that, goes on to believe that these "presentations" are not so much "real" as they are simply "ways" in which we human beings are able to *perceive*

God in the world. In other words, the modalists among us believe that God is not in essence "a three, co-eternal oneness."

Admittedly, there is some re-enforcement or justification for modalism's "oneness" or absolute monotheism position. As Christians, and as we have already acknowledged, we come up and out from the absolute monotheism of our Jewish roots. It follows from that that the monotheism that is so implicit in Christian theology and practice, as well as in Christianity's self-image, understandably is going to have considerable trouble—at least syntactically anyway—with a non-modalist or non-modalist-like Trinity, except, of course, that things are not that simple. They never are. Nor, as far as that is concerned, is the lineage of our inherited monotheism quite so clean and clear-cut as we would like to think.

Sanctus, Sanctus, Sanctus. This, to use the Latin of the medieval church, is how we have praised the Godhead in Christian liturgy for two thousand years, and for very good reason. The reason, however, is not of Christian making.

The author of First Isaiah envisioned the Godhead as being praised by six-winged angels, and it was those angels who first sang the "Holy, Holy, Holy." The frequent reiteration of that glory-filled anthem is still today an essential piece of Jewish liturgy, evoking not only a vocal but also a physical expression. Each time Jews in worship utter the thrice-spoken *kadosh*, they rise up onto the very tips of their toes, thereby symbolizing their desire to join the angels in this most ancient and tri-part song of adoration.

The *Sanctus*, or *kadosh*, while it may be the most aesthetic example of a multifaceted mystery inherent in Jewish monotheism, is hardly the only one, however. In fact, Jewish theologians have argued among themselves for millennia about whether or not Moses actually declared monotheism at Mount Sinai. Was the decree at Sinai monotheism? Did Moses say that there was precisely only one

36

God in existence? Or was it monolatry: Is the Lord simply the God above all others? Even the second of the Ten Commandments might suggest this latter possibility: "You shall have no other gods before me" (Deut. 5:6).

Either way (and the debate, so to speak, goes on), the monotheistic imperative in ancient Judaism remains unmistakable, even if the details of it are slightly beclouded. Certainly the world's other religions all point to the singular Abraham, the founder of the people Israel, as the discoverer of monotheism and the one God.[6]

Christians have, as we know, adopted and adapted Jewish monotheism to their own religious ends for some two thousand years. In 2007, in a video entitled *Everything Is Spiritual*, Rob Bell (at that time the teaching pastor at Mars Hill Bible Church in Grandville, Michigan, and a recognized leader in Emergence Christian thought) produced what is now regarded as a more or less classic expression of the problem for contemporary Christians.

In the clip, Bell, standing before his congregation at Mars Hill, explicates the opening portions of Hebrew Scripture. The first Hebrew word for God in Scripture, he explains, is the one transliterated into English as *Elohim*, a noun that grammatically is either singular or plural, being dependent for its grammatical number upon the verbs and adjectives accompanying it. Bell then begins to review what the first few verses of Genesis say about the activity of this God, pointing out other Hebrew words that describe this God's activity. A minute or so later, he summarizes:

> In verse one, this God is some sort of *creator*; in verse two, this God is some sort of *spirit*; and in verse three, this God is some sort of *word*. This God is one, and yet this God is several. God is some sort of multiple persons, some sort of community of creativity. What a strange way to begin a very, very long book.[7]

He says this last sentence in a slow, dramatic, almost mysterious way. No one can do this quite like Rob Bell, and the whole thing is brilliant in its apparent simplicity.

So this is the present conundrum: Toward whom and for whom are monotheistic Jews rising up onto the tips of their toes as they chant the three-part hymn of the adoring angels? To whom are Trinitarian Christians praying when they pray the *Sanctus* taken out of monotheistic Judaism? Even more foundational, how are we—Christians and Jews alike—to perceive our own beginnings? How should we reverence correctly the God in whose image we hold ourselves to have been fashioned? The only tenable answer is to say that in a Christian context, at least, the Godhead of the Godhead is utterly inexplicable.[8]

But for us and in our times, such a resolution to the problem is no longer possible. Truth be told, it probably never was. Certainly, it can scarcely be adopted as an intellectually honorable position. In effect, the theologically inclined among us, both lay and professional, persist as they have from the beginning because they and/or we have to.[9] The desire to "get behind" the Three in order to analyze how such threeness might interact burns within us.

Perhaps, so the argument goes, by coming to understand that interaction, we will come to understand how the threeness interact(s) with us. That, too, isn't possible, of course, but ironically, as a line of thinking, it always leads, and always has led, to another form or variant of modalism.

To seek after the "inner meaning" of the Trinity by trying to "get behind" the three persons in hope of finding the God "behind" the God leads directly to that fatal other problem inherent in the modalist approach: it makes the Godhead itself into something analogous to a fourth divine being. Thus, first there is the Godhead and then, after that, there are the three personalities whom we perceive and read about in Scripture.

Yet, despite all the words and anxious study and even prayerful pondering, none of this is right and none of this will work. It never has. Midway through his *Enigma Fidei*, old William of St. Thierry himself offered an almost exquisite lament about it all:

> Now, why do I seek what cannot be known in this life? For example, why do I seek to know how the Trinity in heaven can be a unity, or how three can be one; since the Lord and the Apostles and the prophets before them taught that this is the nature of the Lord our God, and added nothing more than this? If the Word and Wisdom of God had wished us to know this in this life, no one could have taught it better in this world than he.[10]

Well said, but not enough to deter William, not enough for the saints before him, and certainly not enough for those of us who, like Rob Bell, are alive and believing in this time of the Great Emergence.

Notes

1. Augustine, *De libero arbitrio* 3.21.60 (authors' translation). We perhaps should also recall here Basil of Caesarea's cautionary comments in his treatise, *On the Holy Spirit*: "Those who are idle in the pursuit of righteousness count theological terminology as secondary" (St. Basil the Great, *On the Holy Spirit*, trans. David Anderson [Crestwood, NY: St. Vladimir's Seminary Press, 1980], 16).

2. Christians have accommodated to these very real dangers over the centuries and, upon occasion, limited doctrinal conversation as a result. One of the best examples of this occurred in 1230 CE, when the Cistercians forbade all sermons on the Feast of the Holy Trinity because they themselves deemed the subject to be too difficult to handle safely or productively.

3. There are no more arresting and sobering words in Holy Writ than those of our Lord on this subject as recorded in Mark 3:28–29 (NKJV): "Assuredly, I say to you, all sins will be forgiven the sons of men, and whatever blasphemies they may utter; but he who blasphemes against the Holy Spirit never has forgiveness, but is subject to eternal condemnation."

4. One of the dangers in brevity is that in trying to be succinct, one can be guilty of broad brush strokes that, lacking nuance, also introduce error into the conversation, however inadvertently. Nowhere is that more obscuring than in situations like this one. While it is true that "fear" can intimidate the faithful

into docile and unanalyzed compliance, it is equally true that genuine and holy fear or awe before the ineffable is a part of Christian living. It is, in fact, one that must never be set aside or lost. There is perhaps no better example of this distinction and its holy use than a prayer first written by John Piper in 2004 and now used on occasion in contemporary cohorts and gatherings when approaching the Trinity. The opening lines of that prayer express elegantly the place of a holy fear in the presence of the unknown. They read thus:

Eternal Father, you never had a beginning. You will never have an ending. You are the Alpha and the Omega. This we believe, because you have revealed it to us. Our hearts leap up with gratitude that you have opened our eyes to see and know that Jesus Christ is your eternal, divine Son, begotten, not made, and that Jesus is the Glory of God. You, O Father, and he, your Son, are one God.

We tremble even to take such glorious truths on our lips for fear of dishonoring you with withering and inadequate words. But we must speak, because we praise you. Silence would shame us, and the rocks themselves would cry out. You must be praised for who you are in the world you have made. And we must thank you because you have made us taste and see the glory of Jesus Christ, your Son. Oh, to know him!

The prayer may be found in its entirety in John Piper, *Seeing and Savoring Jesus Christ* (Wheaton: Crossway, 2004), 25.

5. That great poet and woman of faith/doubt Emily Dickinson also had fun with religion's tendency to trivialize such things in these few, brief, memorable lines imagining God's Spirit at the zoo or the state fair:

A Diagram—of Rapture!
A sixpence at a show
With Holy Ghosts in Cages!

6. The Talmud has Abraham knowing God, the one true Creator, at the age of three. Maimonides, on the other hand, says that it happened when Abraham smashed the idols when he was forty. This story does not appear in any Bible. *Midrash Bereshit* 38:13 adds, as all midrash does, to the scriptural and historical narrative, with the rabbis telling us that Abraham's father was an idol-maker. The story goes like this:

Abraham's father, Terach, was an idol manufacturer. Once he had to travel, so he left Abraham to manage the shop. People would come in and ask to buy idols. Abraham would say, "How old are you?" The person would say, "Fifty," or "Sixty." Abraham would say, "Isn't it pathetic that a man of sixty wants to bow down to a one-day-old idol?" The man would feel ashamed and leave. One time a woman came with a basket of bread. She said to Abraham, "Take this and offer it to the gods." Abraham got up, took a hammer in his hand, broke all the idols to pieces, and then put the hammer in the hand of the biggest idol among them. When his father came back and saw the broken idols, he was appalled. "Who did this?" he cried. "How can I hide anything from you?" replied Abraham calmly.

"A woman came with a basket of bread and told me to offer it to them. I brought it in front of them, and each one said, 'I'm going to eat first.' Then the biggest one got up, took the hammer and broke all the others to pieces." "What are you trying to pull on me?" asked Terach, "Do they have minds?" Said Abraham: "Listen to what your own mouth is saying? They have no power at all! Why worship idols?"

7. Rob Bell, *Everything Is Spiritual* (Grand Rapids: Zondervan, 2007), DVD. Transcription by Tickle and Sweeney.

8. One of the best contemporary quips about all of this was made by one of our most eminent pastors and preachers, Fred Craddock. Craddock is quoted as having, upon occasion, dealt with the problem by telling his seminary students, with tongue in cheek, "I'm not all that interested in the Trinity. I'm more of a Bible person myself"; quoted in Robin R. Meyers, *The Underground Church: Reclaiming the Subversive Way of Jesus* (San Francisco: Jossey-Bass, 2012), 68.

9. Even a historical theologian of the caliber of Bernard McGinn (in the context of discussing the disputes between East and West on the nature of the Trinity) once succumbed to inquiring after "the inner meaning of the Trinity"—as if there is an inner meaning in contrast to an outer or more intelligible meaning. As if one might know something about how the persons of the Trinity understand their *own* unity? Absolutely impossible, of course, but admitting to not knowing is rarely a popular theological solution. See Bernard McGinn, "The Abbot and the Doctors: Scholastic Reactions to the Radical Eschatology of Joachim of Fiore," *Church History*, 40 (1971): 31.

10. William of St. Thierry, *The Enigma of Faith*, trans. John D. Anderson (Kalamazoo, MI: Cistercian Publications, 1973), para. 25, p. 57. It was also William who once said, "To the extent that the divine plan allows itself to be understood, we must eagerly pursue it" (op. cit., para. 1, p. 36). Every serious Christian would probably agree. But then we will always differ in opinion about how much of the divine plan is indeed intended to be understood.

4

The Great Enigma
and Our Grandest Heresy

It was not until 375 CE that the first book or treatise devoted solely and specifically to discussing the nature of the Holy Spirit appeared on the scene. It was written by a bishop in Cappadocia (part of modern Turkey) named Basil, and known to us as Basil of Caesarea or Basil the Great. Basil's little book was titled succinctly, abruptly even, *On the Holy Spirit*. Chapters 1–8 explain the nature of the deity of Christ, after which Basil moves on to argue that the Spirit is equal in the Godhead—clearly, a not yet widely accepted notion:

> We must proceed, now, to attack our opponents as they endeavor to advance opinions which are derived from false knowledge. It is not possible, they say, for the Holy Spirit to be ranked with the Father and Son, on account of the difference of His nature and the inferiority of His dignity. But to them I reply with the words of the apostles: "We ought to obey God rather than any human authority." [Acts 5:29][1]

"Attack our opponents" indeed! Clearly, the early Christian fathers and mothers didn't mess around. But what lay behind Basil's apologia? What was he so agitated about? The answer is Arianism.

Regardless of how colorful Basil of Cappadocia (or how convoluted the stories about him) may have been, there is no question but that Arius, a presbyter in Alexandria, is the heretic whose ideas created the most friction in Basil's own time and, to some extent, have continued to do so right on into ours.[2] Arius, who had lived from ca. 255 CE to 336 CE and quite possibly was not the originator of the heresy that bears his name, had argued that God the Father had created God the Son. If so, then it logically followed that there was a time when God the Son was not. Such a scandalous idea had not been voiced before! A time when God the Father was and God the Son was not? What could that even mean?

First of all and as is often true with most heresies, it meant that Arius had employed Scripture as proof text in an effort to understand. Jesus Himself is recorded in John 14:28 as having said: "You heard me say to you, 'I am going away, and I am coming to you.' If you loved me, you would rejoice that I am going to the Father, because the Father is greater than I." And, like it or not, the Apostle Paul had written to the Corinthians, saying, "Yet for us there is one God, the Father, of whom are all things, and we for Him; and one Lord Jesus Christ, through Whom are all things and through Whom we live" (1 Cor. 8:6 NKJV).

Nothing could be any clearer or more opaque than that. And because Arius's non-co-equal, non-co-eternal understanding of God the Father and God the Son did indeed enjoy some Scriptural validity, it had become the most threatening of the early heresies and the most violently opposed. Almost the whole of the Council of Nicaea in 325 CE was absorbed with discussion of Arius and his ideas.[3] Even the emperor Constantine himself became heavily embroiled in the arguments; and one of the heroes of Trinitarian theology, Athanasius of Alexandria, had his place sealed forever in ecclesial history because of his brilliant opposition to Arian thought.[4]

There were other doctrinal debates and theological movements beside Arianism, of course, almost all of them labeled heretical by some council or congress of churches and almost all of them destined to be freshly considered and reconsidered over the coming centuries. But there was, among the persistent and troubling heresies that originated in Christianity's first half millennium, one that was not about the Trinity in terms of God the Son. Rather, it was about the Trinity in terms of God the Holy Spirit, of how to understand it, and of how to relate to God through it. That one was called Montanism.

Montanism was named for its founder, but Montanus, unfortunately, was a man about whom we know practically nothing other than that he lived in the late second century and was probably from Phrygia in Asia Minor. Whoever he was, though, his ideas were, and are, very clear. He taught that the Holy Spirit was alive and active in the world right here and right now and that the Christian must be constantly attuned to the Spirit's presence and, being attuned by self-discipline and prayer, be ready at all times to perceive and follow the intention or direction of the Spirit. For Montanus, to be fully Christian meant to be receptive to that singular fact with all of one's senses as well as all of one's will and understanding. One had to be intentionally and consciously and actively attuned to the Holy Spirit if one were ever to know what God wanted for one's life.

Unfortunately, original discussions about Montanus and his new doctrine were considerably complicated by his own claims that the Holy Spirit, the *parakletos*,[5] spoke to him and then through him. Such is an audacious claim at any time, but it was especially so in those days of the mid- to late second century, when Christianity was an outlaw faith and Christians could readily be used as fuel for lighting imperial torches or as bait for energizing the games of the amphitheaters. Generally speaking, the whole idea of an inspiriting Holy Spirit seemed fanciful to many, heretical to others, and downright dangerous to everybody. Who knew what this Holy Spirit really was, and who was this Montanus to presume? There were those who said he was possessed by the devil, and there were those who simply ignored him altogether.

Either way, as we all know, his ideas have continued to live on. In fact, they are ideas that, arguably, live more actively now among us than they did in the days of Montanus himself. Arguably, in fact, they were and are the progenitors of Pentecostalism and the first whispers of a faith more spiritual than it is religious.

And Basil would have had something to say to us about that as well. That is, though he was writing his *De Spiritu Sanctu*, his monumental *Of the Holy Spirit*, in 375 CE, he was already acutely aware of the problems that could, and would, arise both from general confusion about the Holy Spirit and also—perhaps most detrimentally—from a natural human reluctance to engage that difficulty at all. "Of the wise men among us," he wrote, "some have conceived of him [i.e., the Holy Spirit] as an activity, some as a creature, some as God, and some have been uncertain which to call him . . . and therefore neither worship him nor treat him with dishonor, but take up a neutral stance." . . . Which diagnosis of the problem is as operative today as it was in Basil's.[6]

Notes

1. These are the opening lines of chap. 10 of Basil of Caesarea's *On the Holy Spirit* (authors' translation).We should note as well that seventeen years before Basil wrote his treatise, Athanasius himself had written a letter to Bishop Serapion to complain about other emerging heresies regarding the Spirit, including that of non-Arian Christians who were, according to Athanasius, "oppos[ing] the Holy Spirit, saying that he is not only a creature, but actually one of the

ministering spirits, and differs from the angels only in degree" (*Creeds, Councils and Controversies: Documents Illustrative of the History of the Church A.D. 337–461*, ed. J. Stevenson [London: SPCK, 1966], 57). Then as now, there was confusion on all sides, in other words.

2. Appendix A gives a brief overview of these major heresies, should the reader wish to pursue them there.

3. Arianism has indeed had a most persistent history, and we would do well to not forget that. As for Arius himself, though he was condemned as a heretic by Nicaea in 325 CE, he was also exonerated a decade later by the First Synod of Tyre in 335 CE. Because the left hand often takes away what the right hand giveth, however, he was posthumously returned to the status of heretic by the First Council of Constantinople in 381 CE.

4. Athanasius, who was later canonized, has, over the centuries, been given many titles by a grateful Church. Thus, he is known in the various communions of the faith as St. Athanasius the Great, or St. Athanasius I of Alexandria, or as St. Athanasius the Confessor. But perhaps the most quixotic thing about the Council of Nicaea and its establishment of an Athanasian, as opposed to an Arian, doctrine of the Trinity as orthodox is the ecclesial legend that St. Nicholas, bishop of Myra and destined to become Santa Claus to millions of children, was so disturbed by Arius's position that he arose from his seat, approached Arius, and then slapped him viciously in the face. So much for the jolly-old-man image.

5. Appendix D elaborates on some half dozen or so Greek words that are used in Christian Scripture to reference or describe the Spirit.

6. Numerous editions and translations of Basil's *De Spiritu Sanctu* are readily available on the internet and elsewhere. This particular translation is one employed by Martha Porter in her stellar workbook/discussion guide, *The Nicene Creed—Ancient Words in the Light of Modern Faith* (Haworth, NJ: St. Johann Press, 2012), 117. Porter also manages to express with great clarity the angst that accrued in Basil's time for all those earnest Christian theologians wrestling with the emerging doctrine of the Holy Spirit. "If One plus One equals One was hard to explain, it became even more difficult when One plus One plus One was still equal to One."

5

Meetings of the Minds

Getting it right. Regardless of Basil the Great's concern about the potential dangers of neutrality in matters of faith, those three words— Getting It Right—when they are strung together in that order, are quite possibly the three most destructive words in human experience. Unquestionably, they are the most devastatingly destructive when they are used by religious people speaking of religious belief.

Getting it right matters terribly—as well it should—to godly people. The problem is that the pursuit of "getting it right" frequently turns godly people into ideological storm troopers, which also is entirely logical, since, as Basil knew, what is being sought and defended is the whole of one's eternity, one's well-being, one's "rightness" with God and with the way things are. Most of us, in fact, who are faith-filled, involved, and thinking people accept the pursuit of rightness as more or less an imperative in human life—a kind of responsibility laid upon us by consciousness itself. The difficulties begin to arise when we feel compelled to codify what we have discerned into that amorphous and shape-shifting thing known as orthodoxy. The uber-difficulty is that, having determined what is orthodox, we then feel compelled to defend to the death what we have codified. *Sic semper est*, as the Romans would say. Thus always it is.

Orthodoxy was an elusive thing in the first dozen or so decades of the Christian movement. From whom and from where, after all, would it come? What we now call the New Testament and recognize as our canon was, in the beginning, nonexistent and, for several decades thereafter, unfixed. Those niggling questions about the God-head that in a few years would become doctrinal issues were at first either unrecognized or else, having been recognized, were allowed to remain in flux. Yet even fairly early on, there was the stirring of a conviction that getting it right was important—very important, in fact. Hear the words of Peter to the early communities:

> Like living stones, let yourselves be built into a spiritual house, to be a holy priesthood, to offer spiritual sacrifices acceptable to God through Jesus Christ. For it stands in scripture: "See, I am laying in Zion a stone, a cornerstone chosen and precious; and whoever believes in him will not be put to shame." To you then who believe, he is precious; but for those who do not believe, "The stone that the builders rejected has become the very head of the corner," and "A stone that makes them stumble, and a rock that makes them fall." They stumble because they disobey the word, as they were destined to do. But you are a chosen race, a royal priesthood, a holy nation, God's own people, in order that you may proclaim the mighty acts of him who called you out of darkness into his marvelous light. (1 Pet. 2:5–9)

The early followers of Jesus were to form a "holy priesthood," to offer "spiritual sacrifices," to build around a "cornerstone," and to be "God's own people." With such metaphors, the matter could not be any clearer, could it?

Of course it could. Those holy ideas had to have body and shape, definitions and specifics. Otherwise, who could possibly know whether he or she was accomplishing them correctly, whether he or she was getting it right?

It would take three centuries, more or less, for the beloved community to translate the almost poetic words of Peter's apostolic letter into a set of normative, authoritative teachings that the Church could use as an acid test of what it meant to be Christian. And that statement—that codification—would come at a huge price.[1]

Christian orthodoxy may fairly be said to have begun in Jerusalem and, more or less, on the morning after Jesus's death. As a kind of proto- or nescient orthodoxy, it resided solely in the hearts and minds of the disciples of Jesus during those first weeks and months. *What did he say that day on the mountain? . . . in the boat? . . . outside of Lazarus's house?* They must have wondered these things among themselves and repeated their remembered answers over and over again to each other. Suddenly, the teachings of their rabbi had taken on an immense importance. Had anyone bothered to write them down?

And then, there was the beginning of that other problem, the one nobody could have foreseen at Calvary, but which was the result of their own enthusiasm, their own sureness that this Jesus was God, and Son of God, and Prince of a different and eternal kingdom. For the first twenty years or so, their beloved community—their close confederacy of Jesus-followers—was primarily, or perhaps exclusively, made up of Jews. Those who believed in the teachings and resurrection of Jesus, being Jews either by birth or by conversion, practiced Christianity within the embrace of their Judaism. It was, for them, as if the rituals and observances of Judaism had simply expanded to admit these more recent additions to its concepts and formalities. But things began to change.

51

Christianity seeped out into a larger world. It seeped in some places, but it was also carried into some other places with evangelizing ardor, albeit carefully and often surreptitiously. The inevitable consequence of the seepage and the proselytizing was that, within just a matter of two or three decades, Christianity fell into the hands and hearts of non-Jews. Jesus-worship became the religion of what some would call "pagans," and the author of Acts referred to as *theosebeis,* "God-reverers" or "God-fearers."[2, 3] Christianity, ready or not, had become the totally embraced faith of goyim who had no truck with food laws and prohibitions, who had never seen a rabbi and did not particularly ever want to, and who most definitely had no interest in circumcision, either as a religious rite or otherwise.

It was apparent to all that Jerusalem had a problem, that the beloved community had a problem. Were these Gentiles, these pagans, really Christians or merely look-alikes and wannabes? Every evidence of genuine belief was there in their lives and their conduct. Even the Spirit seemed to be guiding them and revealing God to them and engaging them in the exact same ways that were happening in Jerusalem among the beloved community. Yet these non-Jewish believers were clearly not observing the whole sum of what the fathers and elders and apostles had understood as normative, as necessary, even. Was the uncircumcised brother really a brother? Could he possibly be? And, most poignant of all, if he were, then who is right? Which of us has heard God correctly, for we cannot both be right and maintain such contradictory stances, can we?

The issues grew, and with them the tensions of rightness among godly people, both Jewish and pagan. The result was what is now known as the Jerusalem Conference, though it hardly had so august a naming originally. What it had was much humbler than that. Originally, that is, it was simply a gathering of early Christian leaders from around the eastern Mediterranean world, coming together to meet in the epicenter of first-century Judaism. It was around the year 50 CE, and they had been called there by the Jerusalem community to determine one thing only: Did a Gentile have to become a Jew, through ritual circumcision and other adherences to the Law, in order to be a follower of Jesus? Or, put another way, to be a Christian, did one necessarily also have to live and practice as a Jew?[4]

The two pillars of the movement, Paul of Tarsus and that intimate disciple of Jesus, Simon Peter, debated this issue before the others who were assembled there. Today we have only two texts—both in the New Testament, and nothing else—depicting that moment in time. The first one to be published was Paul's own account, retained now in Galatians, chap. 2. The second appeared some fifteen to twenty years later, written anonymously, and appears in the Acts of the Apostles, chap. 15.

In summary, what the Jerusalem Conference determined was that Gentiles were welcomed into the movement and were no longer required to undergo circumcision. They were, however, expected to follow many of the ethical and spiritual practices that set first-century Jews apart from their Roman counterparts. That is, they were instructed to spurn idol worship, steer clear of sexual immorality, and refrain from eating animal flesh still mixed with blood. In sum, though they did not have to go under the knife, they still had to listen to Moses.

In the years immediately following the Jerusalem Conference, the first followers of Jesus who had gathered there began, with greater intention than ever, to broadcast their Gospel. After 50 CE and Jerusalem, they were to spread themselves and their message throughout the Roman world within a matter of only a decade or two. Yet even as they traveled, settled, and resettled, they continued to have the theological and ecclesial chores of trying to create a language capable of conveying the fullness of their new rituals and celebrations, worship and beliefs. Among other things, the Christian way-of-being that was rapidly morphing out of first-century Judaism had to create a canon of its own, a body of Holy Scriptures, a fixity by which rightness in matters of belief and action could be determined.[5]

The process of discovery ground on for well over two centuries until, as we have already seen and as is the nature of such things, certain doctrinal issues became impossible to avoid. Even among those Jesus communities that strove to focus on practice over doctrine, the issues—and most especially the central, pivotal issues concerning the nature of Jesus's being—could no longer be shoved under the communal rug. How does one, for example, explain that Jesus was fully God and fully man, all at once? How does one understand that Jesus is God despite the recorded fact that, as Arius so emphatically continued to point out, He seemed to defer, at times, to His Father in heaven? How, for that matter, does one explain or even conceive of three Gods in one? Their Jewish grandfathers and grandmothers in the Jesus way had never had these problems.

What those early Jewish forebears had had, however, was the Jerusalem Conference. Jerusalem had set, if not an arbitrary norm, then at least the only extant model of how to discuss issues correctly, especially potentially divisive ones. As we have seen, it was time now for the world's Christian leaders to gather once again. The year was 325 CE, and their gathering at Nicaea would become known to later history as both the Council of Nicaea and the First Ecumenical Council of the Church. It was the "Ecumenical" part of that wording that would come to matter almost as much as the place name of Nicaea.

Notes

1. See, most notably, Walter Bauer, *Orthodoxy and Heresy in Earliest Christianity* (Philadelphia: Fortress, 1971), and Rowan Williams, "Does It Make Sense to Speak of Pre-Nicene Orthodoxy?" in *The Making of Orthodoxy: Essays*

in Honour of Henry Chadwick, ed. Rowan Williams (New York: Cambridge University Press, 1989).

2. This should not be interpreted as meaning, as is so often assumed, that Christianity had come among the godless. It had not. In fact, things might have been easier or clearer had the so-called pagans been without prior religious beliefs and practice. It was, instead, the very presence of those operative beliefs and practices that offered the young Church a considerable number of obstacles. There is perhaps no better way to grasp this difficulty than to hear what Maximus of Tyre had to say on the issue of contemporary religious belief.

A second-century philosopher who was typical of his sophist colleagues in his very Greek and very Platonic view of the meaning of God and gods, Maximus left us this summary of the religious tenor of his times: "The one doctrine upon which all the world is united is that one God is king of all and father, and that there are many gods, sons of God, who rule together with God. This is believed by both the Greek and the barbarian" (Maximus of Tyre, *Origen: Contra Celsum*, trans. with an introduction and notes by Henry Chadwick [New York: Cambridge University Press, 1980], xvii).

3. Should the reader wish to pursue the matter of *theosebeis* further and in its biblical context, the words of the Apostle Paul on the subject may be found in Acts 13:16 and 13:26. For a brief secondary source on the same topic, the reader may wish to see Diarmaid MacCulloch's monumental *Christianity: The First Three Thousand Years* (New York: Penguin Books, 2011), 99, or, for a more in-depth study, J. Brian Tucker's "God-fearers: Literary Foil or Historical Reality in the Book of Acts?," *Journal of Biblical Studies* 5, no. 1 (2005): 21–39.

4. Genesis 17:14 had clearly stated that only circumcised males could be God's people.

5. Interestingly enough, both the Jewish and Christian canons were being formed almost simultaneously, as it were. The Torah, of course, had been long since set in stone, but Jews of the late second and early third centuries CE were still busy trying to establish which of the prophets and minor books were to be added to it as canonical Scripture. At about the same time, Christians were beginning their own exercise of discerning which Gospels were in, which letters were truly written by Paul, and what other documents were to be deemed inspired by the disciples of Christ or the communities that formed immediately around them.

6

A Confusion of Creeds

By whatever name one wishes to call it, it was at Nicaea that Christianity arrived for the first time at a clear, intentional, self-conscious definition of what it was. The first edition of what we know now as the Nicene Creed was rendered there by reasoned debate and adopted by consensus. Christian orthodoxy had at last been born, but so too had the difficulties attendant on orthodoxy, for the wary relationship between truth and power in Christian affairs had been exposed beyond undoing at Nicaea. Constantine had failed completely in his efforts to disguise his intention to foist theological unity upon the gathered bishops not for the sake of the Church so much as for the purpose of solidifying an empire and, thereby, his imperial strength.

A half century later, there was a Second Ecumenical Council. There would be seven such councils over the coming four and a half centuries, and it would take almost fifty years of contentious discussion before the convocation of this second of them was even necessary. But convene it did, in 381 CE, when the bishops and theologians of the Church gathered at Constantinople for the specific purpose of looking again at the creed as it had been established at Nicaea. The changes put in place at Constantinople as a result of that gathering may appear, if they are only superficially scanned, to have been minor—more doctoring words than substance. But there are no minor adjustments in matters of religion.

Every addition and subtraction put into place at the Second Council was believed to be critical by those gathered there. As a result, what we today so cavalierly call the Nicene Creed is really more correctly referred to as the Niceno-Constantinopolitan Creed. Regardless of its having a formal and more specific name, though, what most of us refer to in ordinary conversation as the Nicene Creed is not the original creed but rather the adjusted one that came out of that Second Ecumenical Council. Thus, with the modifications and additions printed in bold italics, Constantinople gave us these very familiar words:

We believe in One God, the Father Almighty, maker *of heaven and earth, and* of all things visible and invisible.

And in one Lord Jesus Christ, the *only-begotten* Son of God, begotten of the Father *before all worlds*;

Light of Light; true God of true God; begotten, not made; of one essence with the Father, by whom all things were made; who for us men and for our salvation came down from heaven, and was incarnate *by the Holy Spirit of the Virgin Mary*, and became man.

He was crucified for us under Pontius Pilate, and suffered, *and was buried.*

And the third day He arose again, *according to the Scriptures, and* ascended into Heaven, *and sits at the right hand of the Father*; and He shall come again *with glory* to judge the living and the dead; *whose kingdom shall have no end.*

And in the Holy Spirit, *the Lord, the Giver of Life, Who proceeds from the Father; Who with the Father and the Son together is worshipped and glorified; Who spoke by the prophets.*

And in one, holy, catholic, and apostolic Church.
We acknowledge one baptism for the remission of sins.
We look for the resurrection of the dead, and the life of the
world to come.

Obviously there are a number of things being asserted here, but for the purposes of our present discussion, one is of most particular importance. Now, at last, the Holy Spirit has been given an official role. Or, perhaps more discreetly said: the struggle to grasp in words what the Holy Spirit is and does has now arrived at creedal proportions.

By any stretch of rhetorical imagination, there is no way to unsay the fact that the Second or Constantinople Council in 381 CE made Jesus of Nazareth the direct product or result or effected consequence of an act of the Holy Spirit. In some ways, and in ways that would arguably become even more significant in our Emergence times, the Holy Spirit is now reverenced as the giver of all life, the voice of the prophets, and a procession of the Father.[1] These, in other words, were not merely linguistic adjustments and accommodations! They were substantive changes that mattered then and have mattered for all the centuries since.

Any real understanding today of the progression of ideas and concepts that led from the Creed of Nicaea to the Creed of the Second Ecumenical Council must rest, ultimately, upon at least a modicum of understanding about a group of three men known to history as the Cappadocian Fathers. We have already met one of them, Basil of Caesarea. The other two in that pivotal trio were Basil's brother, Gregory of Nyssa, and their mutual friend, Gregory of Nazianzus.

All three men were brilliant, but they were also deeply devout and persuaded Christians. In their brilliance and their faithfulness, as well as in the ardor of their concerns, they paved the way in the years between Nicaea and First Constantinople (i.e., the Second

Ecumenical Council) for a more studied and careful articulation of the Trinitarian God. In particular, the Church owes the Cappadocians great gratitude for their conceptualization or definition of the Trinity as "three-in-oneness."

At First Nicaea, Constantine had chosen, and then championed, a Greek noun, *homoousios*, as the proper tool with which to describe the nature of the Son and thereby to counter Arius and his "heresy" of Son as less than Father. *Homoousios* itself is a melding of two Greek semantic units: *homo*, meaning "same," and *ousios*, meaning something analogous to our English words "essence" or "substance." By employing it, Constantine and the theologians and churchmen allied with him had sought to describe the Son as "same in being or substance" with and to the Father.

The churchmen and theologians in the eastern part of the empire and Church were, from the very first, uneasy with this solution, however, and for good reason. *Homoousios* was not innocent of doctrinal history. It had been used over half a century earlier by Paul of Samosate. A deposed Syrian bishop of Antioch, Paul had employed *homoousios* as part of his promulgation of the Monarchian heresy, which held that God was one and one only, the King of all. Jesus, by this line of argument, was a man who became God at His baptism in the Jordan River. Nonetheless, and despite the history-based objections of the Eastern bishops, Constantine had insisted; and what the emperor wanted, the emperor usually got. Certainly he did in this case, anyway; and after Nicaea, *homoousios*, already tainted, entered everyday liturgical usage as a way to describe the Father and the Son. They were to be understood as being of one substance.

Over the years after 325 CE and before Constantinople in 381 CE, however, the distinctiveness of the members of the Trinity had seemed to many Christians to somehow be dissolving, if not coming increasingly into outright question. It was the Cappadocian Fathers who found the way forward by creating the language that would thereafter be used to explain what they called three-in-oneness.

Up until the Cappadocians in the middle of the fourth century, little distinction had been made in Greek between the word *ousia* and the word *hypostasis*. Both were used to denote what we in English would call "essence" or "being." Basil and the two Gregorys changed this. They began to write voluminously on the subject, in fact, persuading bishops and theologians all over the Christian world that the two words should be understood not as synonyms, but as referencing distinctly different constructs.

Borrowing from some of the ideas of Aristotle, the Cappadocians argued that the understanding of this difference between *ousia* and *hypostasis* is itself a holy work, especially and inasmuch as that distinction—however fine and torturous it might be—offered the explanation for what the Cappadocians saw as being the world's greatest mystery. The Trinity, they said, is, in fact, one *ousia* (or "essence") and three *hypostases* (or "individuals"; this concept would eventually be renamed as "persons").

This distinction on the part of Basil and the two Gregorys has endured now for centuries. No small part of that longevity lies in the fact that, as a solution, it deftly avoids polytheism as well as Jewish monotheism. Basil himself understood this, almost turning those categories on their heads in the process when he wrote:

> It is indispensable to have clear understanding that, as he who fails to confess the community of the essence (*ousia*) falls into polytheism so he who refuses to grant the distinction of the *hypostases* is carried away into Judaism.[2]

But shortly after the Cappadocians had successfully made their point, it became the Western bishops' turn to be troubled over a specific word. Basically, the whole thing was a simple matter of Western Latin's distorting the meaning of the Eastern Fathers' Greek, but that point seems to have been lost in the fourth-century fray.

The word *hypostasis*, defined most literally, means "foundation" or "sediment." It was heard, however, as something rather different (and very troubling) by the bishops and theologians in the West, many of whom rarely understood Greek nuances and subtleties.

When Roman ecclesial translators took *hypostasis* over into Latin, they rendered the Greek prefix *hypo-* into the Latin one of *sub-*, a not unreasonable rendering had the whole exercise been merely a matter of *hypo-* and *sub-* as freestanding linguistic elements. But they were not; each was but a member-part or prefix to a larger word. The unfortunate consequence was that, when the Greek *stasis* became the Latin *stantia*, there was a lack of linguistic equivalency, which is a polysyllabic way of saying that there was trouble, and *hypo-stasis* became a "sub-stance." Compounding one misunderstanding upon another, when the East then spoke of God as having three of these *hypostases*, the West heard it as three substances, and that simply could not be! That would be tritheism!

Blessedly, by the time the Second Ecumenical Council (or First Council of Constantinople, if one prefers that name) was actually convened in 381 CE, much of the misunderstanding had been either cleared up or, at least to some extent, ameliorated. Indeed, several centuries later and most beautifully, one of the inheritors of the Cappadocians' wisdom, St. Symeon the New Theologian, would be able to describe the Trinity as "triple light in unity but unique light in three."[3] Or more mundanely, but perhaps more clearly, "The Trinity . . . is one 'what' and three 'who's.'"[4]

There is one other point that must not be overlooked here, though it may seem incidental initially: every important creedal decision in the opening centuries of the Christian era was made at an ecumenical gathering of the world's Christian leaders. "Ecumenical" meant worldwide; it meant West and East, both. And "gathering" meant what it said: governance and decision by a coming together. The Jerusalem Conference had set the precedent, and that precedent was to be followed precisely for four centuries.[5]

Notes

1. Even four years before the Second Ecumenical Council, a Roman consul, in a condemnation of the heresy known as Apollinarianism, would declare: "As men who hold fast through everything to the inviolable faith of the council of Nicaea, we do not separate the Holy Spirit, but together with the Father and the Son we offer him a joint worship as complete in everything, in power, honor, majesty and Godhead" (*Creeds, Councils and Controversies: Documents Illustrative of the History of the Church A.D. 337–461*, ed. J. Stevenson [London: SPCK, 1966], 88).

2. Basil of Caesarea, "Basil on the Doctrine of the Trinity, 375," *Creeds, Councils and Controversies*, 122.

3. St. Symeon the New Theologian, *Hymns of Divine Love*, trans. George A. Maloney (Denville, NJ: Dimension, 1976), 39.

4. Scot Douglass, *Theology of the Gap: Cappadocian Language Theory and the Trinitarian Controversy* (New York: Peter Lang, 2007), 2n1.

5. While a detailed discussion of the seven ecumenical councils is not requisite here, the interested reader may want to see Appendix B for a listing and brief annotated overview of them.

7

A Tintack and the
Mighty Machine

From the early days of the Church to our own, it is the Trinity that consistently has been examined and then re-examined by the Church, defined and codified, only to later be undefined and re-codified all over again. It is, and for centuries has been, the Trinity and the nature, function, action, and definition of It that have been ripped apart, argued over, fought over, even killed over; for when all is said and done, it is Trinity that is the core of Christianity and upon which all authority must therefore be established and in which all understanding must be rooted. And the problem with all of this is that the Church really never has known what the Trinity is.

Patrick Leigh Fermor, Britain's great travel writer of the last century, known for his lengthy asides on Byzantine art and Orthodoxy's lost theological treasures, once called the *filioque* the "tintack which split Christendom."[1] So it was and, like it or not, so it continues to be even now fifty some years since Fermor made his caustic observation.

The problem with all of this is that while most of us know what a tintack is, we, up until quite recently, have managed to be happily unconcerned with what the *filioque* is. Truth told, in fact, most of us in Western or latinized Christianity didn't know, also until quite recently, that there was such a thing even to be ignorant of.

A tintack is that humblest of all nails, and perhaps one of the oldest of them as well, not to mention its having been the forebear of our own rather plebian thumbtack. It is a lightweight fastener beaten or shaped out of lightweight metal and destined to be lightweight in the burden it tacks together. It should, in other words, be of no consequence unless, perchance, it should fall out of its place and directly into the working gears of a mighty machine, which, as Fermor observed, is exactly what this one did.

The mighty machine was, is, and for two millennia has been, the Church. As for the *filioque*, it is just a simple Latin word—or, to be a bit more accurate, when translated into English, it is just a simple phrase. In either case, it means "and from the Son."[2] It dropped into the mighty machine in the year of our Lord 689 when it fell—ah, most would now say was intentionally, if furtively, dropped—into the working gears of the machine. That is, 689 CE was the year when *filioque* was inserted by the churchmen and power brokers of the Latin-speaking Church into the Church Universal's greatest statement of faith, the Nicene Creed, thereby making either two creeds or two variants of one creed, depending on one's point of view.

Either way, within the Latin-speaking half of the Church, what, before 689 CE, had read as:

Credo in unum Deum, Patrem omnipotentem. . . . Et in Spiritum Sanctum, Dominum, et vivicantem; qui ex Patre procedit

I believe in one God, the Father Almighty. . . . And in the Holy
Spirit, the Lord, the giver of life, who proceeds from the Father

after 689 CE became:

Credo in unum Deum, Patrem omnipotentem. . . . Et in Spiritum
Sanctum, Dominum, et vivicantem; qui ex Patre Filioque *procedit*

I believe in one God, the Father Almighty. . . . And in the Holy
Spirit, the Lord, the giver of life, who proceeds from the Father
and the Son.

A tintack had just changed the very definition of the Trinity, and
by extension, of God.

A simple word, even one that admittedly had been slipped into
things under the cover of night so to speak, should not, logically
speaking, have created much more than a creedal hiccup of sorts.
Or it would not have done much more than that in our time. But the
seventh century was not our time, nor was the world of its citizens
like ours.

In that distant era, the words of Scripture were heard but hardly
ever seen. The typical Christian never, in his or her whole lifetime,
glimpsed the pages of a Bible with his or her own eyes. Not in
church, not at home, never. Scriptures were mentioned in sermons and read from lecterns, usually in languages unfamiliar to
many of those gathered there to listen. Phrases from Scripture
were embedded in liturgies that were spoken by the faithful or
chanted by a distant choir, but there was no understanding of the
Bible as a book that was accessible or even as something to be read
for oneself. Liturgy was everything. The words and phrases of liturgy—such as those said aloud by the faithful in the Creed—were
the full meaning of faith and the transport of heaven to earth. It

was those words—those words of the people's faith—that had been inexplicably changed.

What happened when the *Spiritum Sanctum* ceased to proceed just *ex Patre* and abruptly (or so it must have seemed to Latin-speaking laity) was said to proceed both *ex Patre* and *ex Filio* (i.e., *filioque*) was a diminishment of the Holy Ghost. It was a clear signal that the Spirit was somehow "less" than the Son, since the greater cannot proceed from the lesser. Rather, the greater gives rise to the lesser.

It was a subtle but telling change. It was also a power play on the part of the political and ecclesial leaders of the West who first suggested and then enforced it. And in a way, settling on an understanding of the Spirit as a quasi-weapon or serious token in a political and cultural tussle had its own kind of logic. The Spirit cannot be controlled, neither there and then nor here and now. Likewise, the Spirit does not have any trail or history or definition that can be manipulated by human interpretation, much less stabilized by clerical rhetoric. The Son was a different matter. The Son was present in physical history and had been defined to some greater or lesser degree in physical documents that require the skills of informed and powerful men if they are to be correctly read and interpreted, of course, but still legitimate and tangible artifacts.

Yes, the Spirit was an outlier and not a team player in the game of building institutions, and by 689 CE there was quite definitely a whole organization of coaches and managers in the western half of the old Roman Empire who were seriously into the business of building institutions and who therefore needed team players and only team players. Free thinkers and loose agents were dangerous to the stability of both the Church and the State in those perilous times. The *filioque* was to be a further enforcement and guarantee of that stability. Thus it is that to this very day, we still refer to our tintack by its dogmatic name of "the double procession of the Holy Ghost." What an ominous-sounding thing that is.

Any thinking person, especially any thinking Christian, would, and should, be tempted to say right about now that perhaps we would be better off if we just chose to walk away from that disingenuous moment in our history, as well as from its precursors and its sequelae. Perhaps we would be better off, after all, just to let it be. Certainly that great historian of Christianity Jaroslav Pelikan thought so. He famously once observed that:

> If there is a special circle of the inferno described by Dante reserved for historians of theology, the principal homework assigned to that subdivision of Hell for at least the first several eons of eternity may well be a thorough study of all the treatises . . . devoted to the inquiry: Does the Holy Spirit proceed from the Father only, as Eastern Christendom contends, or from both the Father and the Son as the Latin Church teaches?[3]

What, indeed, could possibly be the purpose of investigating today matters that seem to have been both a bit unsettling for centuries and yet of little consequence now? What could be the point of such, other than as an intellectual exercise? What is to be gained by the expenditure of so much energy in investigating an old and odd collection of ecclesial and doctrinal shenanigans? Unfortunately, the answer is: Quite a bit, especially if one reads either the tea leaves or the daily news.

The truth of the thing, in other words, is that we can't walk away from the *filioque* story, and not just because there is a good, if sometimes scurrilous, set of tales to be told here. Rather, we can no longer walk away from the *filioque* because those interweaving and sometimes disturbing stories that are its history are also suddenly, wrenchingly pertinent to the present and future of this thing we call Church. In sum, we are stuck with it, like it or not.

How that tintack change in the Church's earlier days unravels and is unraveled in our time concerns every person on the planet who today adopts the name of Christ. It especially concerns those of us who are latinized or Northern Hemisphere, Western Christians for several subtle and two fairly obvious reasons.

Ours is a shrinking world, literally. Barriers and inconveniences and delays in communications that once seemed an incontestable and natural part of how the world worked no longer apply. Ugly as the word may sound to the ear, "glocalization" is our reality now. The nation, the continent, the indigenous culture, the hemisphere are all reduced to a kind of antique or quaint status of remembrance. And Christendom has glocalized along with the rest of the world.

The balance of influence in Christendom no longer rests in the so-called First World, nor in Euro-Caucasian demographics. The bulk of Christians live elsewhere now and, even if that were not true, they now have ready access to and empowered influence in the world's theological debates and ecclesial discussions. The descendants of the Western churchmen who needed and then asserted the *filioque* no longer command the influence their forebears did. More to the point, the Spirit, whose mysterious lack of definition was treasured and worshipped by Eastern and Orthodox Christians, now moves across the waters and blows within the currents of the wind. We can call that shift by names like Pentecostalism or the Charismatic movement, or we can recognize it as a major characteristic of Emergence Christianity, or we can use it to explain the phenomenon of the "spiritual but not religious." But none of those things changes the fact that, ready or not, we have come into the Age of the Spirit.

Notes

1. Patrick Leigh Fermor, *Between the Woods and the Water: On Foot to Constantinople—The Middle Danube to the Iron Gates* (New York: New York Review of Books, 2005), 197.

2. *-que* is actually a construct attached to the end of a Latin word to indicate what English indicates by the word *and*. *Filio-* is a prepositional form of *filius*, the Latin word for *son*. All of which is how, in translation, *filioque* becomes *and from the Son*.

3. Jaroslav Pelikan, *The Melody of Theology: A Philosophical Dictionary* (Cambridge, MA: Harvard University Press, 1988), 90.

8

The Conversation Redux

Clichés are like old garden shoes: seriously worn, almost always covered in muddy experience, yet enormously appropriate and economical when one is working a piece of ground. And, at the moment, there could be no more appropriate way for us to proceed than to use the weary old saw that holds that "whatever goes around comes around." As clichés go, that one is almost always unfailingly accurate, and Lord knows, it certainly is in this case.

While our generalized fascination with human subjectivity, psychological phenomena, and interior experience may be a relatively new trend or focus in Western culture and popular conversation, concern about the Spirit per se certainly is not. The Spirit out there somewhere, the Spirit as entity within a Godhead that is both with and without entities, that objectified Spirit—that Spirit—has indeed been a source of varying levels of concern, especially among theologians, fathers and mothers of the Church, and secular and ecclesial authorities from the very beginning of Christianity.

What had seemed at first to be little more than a cache of mixed Scriptural signals had grown, by the time of Montanus and his ghostly heresies of the mid-second century CE, into heated discussions— or were all of those conversations about the imperative that good Christian folk should attend constantly to the Holy Spirit as ranging and directive in present time really heretical? Some were, and some weren't, of course, and the trick for many centuries to come was going to be the prayerful winnowing out of the wheat from the chaff.

By the early fourth century and the convoking of the First Ecumenical Council at Nicaea, some of those earliest heated discussions had matured into the perceived need, as we have seen, for creedal clarity about the Trinity, about Jesus as Son, and about the Holy Spirit as who knew what. Blessedly, God the Father seemed, at that point in time anyway, to be fairly securely fixed in a position or role that needed no further defining.

But few religious creeds or declarations of orthodoxy, be they Christian or otherwise, are ever free from debate for very long— earnest, and often contentious, debate. That certainly, as we know, was the case with Nicaea, and it eventuated in 381 CE in the convening of the Second Ecumenical Council of the Church in Constantinople where the original Nicene Creed of 325 CE was modified and expanded to clarify, among other things, what exactly was to be understood by faithful believers about the nature and function of the Holy Spirit. But the subterranean rumblings continued and grew in magnitude for another half century when, in 431 CE, the Third Ecumenical Council was convened in Ephesus. And it was Canon 7 of the Council of Ephesus that made it an "unfaithful, unkind, and spiritually treasonous act" for anyone to bring forward or write or compose any other creed as a rival to the one that was defined by the holy fathers who were gathered together in the Holy

Spirit at Nicaea. By which those gathered actually meant the Niceno-Constantinopolitan Creed, but no matter. The point had been made and was very clear.

All that "unfaithful, unkind, and spiritually treasonous" wording was still not formidable enough, however, to restrain godly men and women from continuing to mull upon some foundational concerns. A kind of nescient but growing awareness of *filioque*—of double procession of the Holy Spirit from both the Father and the Son—as a correct, defensible, and/or perhaps even requisite doctrine or understanding was, if not roiling, then at least simmering in Latin conversation. It was, in point of fact, being debated in theological circles, even as Ephesus met. Admittedly, much of the conversation was a bit *sotto voce*, but that did not make it any less sincere and portentous.

Three verses from the New Testament, in particular, were most often used in those early debates as support for the idea of "double procession."

In his Letter to the Philippians, Paul writes, "for I know that through your prayers and the help of the Spirit of Jesus Christ this will turn out for my deliverance" (Phil. 1:19). In writing to his friend Titus, Paul says, "This Spirit he poured out on us richly through Jesus Christ our Savior" (Titus 3:6). And whoever the man or woman who wrote Luke-Acts may have been, he or she had this to say about Christ: "Being therefore exalted at the right hand of God, and having received from the Father the promise of the Holy Spirit, he has poured out this that you both see and hear" (Acts 2:33).

Of course, despite the fact that each of these passages seemed to argue for the addition of *filioque* and the hierarchal arrangement of double procession within the Trinity, there were—and almost always are—contrary proof texts. In the case of the *filioque*, Eastern or Greek-speaking Christians tended then—and have continued since—to be exquisitely attuned to those contrary texts for some reason. Consider, for example, these words of Jesus taken from John's Gospel:

> When the Advocate comes, whom I will send to you from the Father, the Spirit of truth who comes from the Father, he will testify on my behalf. (15:26)

Even the Lord himself seems to say here that the Spirit proceeds from the Father alone. Or, barring that, the most one can surmise from his words is the possible option of the Spirit's coming from the Father *through* the Son (certainly not *and from* the Son!). In any event, one or the other of those two options was to inform for centuries the position of theologians in the East who deeply opposed the West's increasing insistence upon *filioque*, with its apparent diminishment of the Holy Spirit as an essential adjustment to the creed.

And so it was that, by the late seventh century CE, Nicaea, Ephesus, and all the heated discussions associated with them had devolved into outright ecclesial warfare, and the *filioque* was quietly maneuvered into place as part of the Western Church's recitation of the Nicene Creed. The tintack had been dropped into the mighty machine.

It had all been done so cleverly, so very, very cleverly. In one stroke of the pen, Western or Latin Christianity managed to change the definition of the Spirit simply by changing the nature of relationships within the Trinity. The oldest and noblest of the Church's creeds, the Nicene, had been modified subtly but profoundly by half the body of Christ on earth. Where once all Christians—both Eastern and Western—murmured, "I believe in . . . the Holy Spirit, the Lord, the giver of life, who proceeds from the Father," now half of them, both clergy and laity, were permitted and even encouraged by Mother Church upon occasion to murmur, "I believe in . . . the Holy Spirit, the Lord, the giver of life, who proceeds from the Father and the Son." *Filioque.*

It first happened in a most ordinary sort of way in one of the medieval world's more out-of-the-way places. It first happened at Toledo in Spain in 589 CE. At that time and in that part of the old empire, Latin Christianity was deeply embroiled in the clarifying business of converting some recalcitrant followers of Arius to more acceptable, more Athanasian ways of believing. In their struggle to stamp out Arianism completely and finally in Spain, the bishops in Toledo inserted the *filioque* into the Creed. What the bishops gained by making that insertion was, of course, creedal proof that the Son was indeed God and had been from the beginning and, from that position of co-being, had been that from which the Spirit had proceeded. It followed logically that, in order to establish the absolute immutability of their change, the bishops had to make their insertion of the *filioque* into the law of the land as well as of the Sabbath mass.

Anathemas against Arius and his doctrines and his miscreant adherents would henceforth march in lockstep with that one, single, danger-fraught word that had been so shrewdly—and so very, very arbitrarily—added to the Niceno-Constantinopolitan Creed by bishops acting on their own regional authority. Perhaps, though, and to give them their due, we should admit the possibility that the bishops and churchmen present at Toledo in 589 CE never actually intended to create a discontinuity with the past.[1] But whether intended or not, that disconnect happened among them and by their hand. More than that, from Toledo onward, every time Arian Christians were identified and confronted throughout the centuries of medieval Europe, they were forced to acknowledge and then speak the *filioque*. It had become, for much of Europe, the litmus test of choice.

Despite the intrusion of the *filioque* into European affairs after 589 CE and despite its repeated use in letters from Latin popes to Orthodox patriarchs and back again, and despite the theological ping-pong that took place among monks and academics for the next four-hundred-plus years—despite all those things—leaders of the two branches of the church, East and West, popes in Rome and patriarchs in Constantinople, largely avoided the major landmines buried just below the surface of their differences. In fact, they stepped lightly around and over them for a while, because the use and practice of the *filioque* did not immediately go into uniform practice everywhere or consistently.

But if the *filioque* as official doctrine did not enjoy a highly visible inception or a particularly appealing initial *raison d'être*, it most surely has not enjoyed an innocuous or very quiet existence since. From the first, it seemed destined, like everything that goes around, to indeed come around again, and again, and again.[2] Prior to our own time in history, it was to make its most dramatic appearance in 1054 CE when, among other things, it would cause a world war, or at the very least, when it would become the ordained excuse for one, as well as the ultimate symbol of the differences being settled by one. Both the Church and formal history would call that deadly engagement the Great Schism. It would become the third of the seismic, semi-millennial shifts Christianized culture has gone through since we changed our dating of eras from BCE to CE.[3]

The Great Schism is traditionally and continually memorialized in seminary courses as having taken place in the year 1054, but as every historian worth his or her salt will tell you, it was actually sealed as inevitable for all practical purposes forty years earlier, in 1014. February 14, 1014, to be specific, was the month, day, and year when the new Holy Roman Emperor, a Bavarian who took the title Henry II, decreed that Benedict VIII, the bishop of Rome who had just crowned him, must begin reciting the Nicene Creed with the *filioque* on certain occasions and for special events. It was so simple, so innocuous, so subtle-as-a-snake easy.

The truth of the thing is that, despite the Eastern Church's plainly and frequently stated opposition to double procession—or perhaps because of it, some would say—a goodly number of Western emperors had already pressured Rome over the preceding years since Toledo to command the insertion of *filioque* into the Latin mass. There was no doubt in anybody's mind that the emperors' desires had very little to do with theology but instead had a great deal to do with power plays and demarcating the areas and reach of their own governance. It took Pope Benedict VIII, however, to finally do what was asked of him by imperial power.

Benedict VIII and Henry II of Bavaria were made for each other. In an era when it was rare for a pope and an emperor to share much affection for one another, these two were inextricably bound by circumstance and, quite possibly, by a certain large dedication to expediency in both their personalities. However, all of that may have been, it is absolutely true that Benedict owed his very life to Henry.

In 1012, Benedict VIII, at that point only recently crowned as pope, had been forced to flee from Rome rather hastily. The supporters of Gregory VI, an antipope and false pretender to the chair of St. Peter, were threatening his very life. But Henry II, who at the time was only king of Bavaria and not yet Holy Roman Emperor, used his sword and his considerable military force to slash the way open for Benedict's return. He did so with the understanding, of course, that Benedict would one day return the favor.[4] And so it was that two years later, on St. Valentine's Day, 1014 CE, Benedict VIII placed the crown of the Holy Roman Emperor upon Henry II's head at St. Peter's Basilica and, in compliance with Henry's express wishes, had the *filioque* included in the coronation masses.

In the naves of churches on that February morning, and assuming they were paying attention, Christians throughout the Eternal City heard *filioque* intoned for the first time, but the soft sounds of its chanting were hardly whispered before they were heard as a roar around all of the Christian world. East and West

had entered into the final stages of coming undone one from another. They had fallen asunder. After that, the Great Schism itself
came rather quickly.

Only forty years later, the unspeakable, the irreparable, and the
unthinkable happened. Pope Leo IX, through his emissaries, excommunicated the Eastern patriarch, Michael Cerularius of Constantinople. In response, the patriarch immediately anathematized the
pope. It was over.

We have come a thousand years since then and, indeed, stand now
within the time of the Great Schism's millennial anniversary.[5] We
have come as well to a time in the world's history that is characterized, among other things, by a process of rapid internationalization.
Schisms, whether ecclesial or geo-political—assuming there is a
distinction to be made between those two—cannot be allowed to go
unattended and unameliorated. Accordingly, in the face of different
circumstances and vastly different priorities, both the Church and
the State have expended considerable effort over the last half century or so in trying to undo what had been done centuries ago. The
Eastern and Western Churches, both caught in a shrinking world,
must discover a basis for, at the very least, the public appearance
of common cause in an increasingly non-Christian milieu. It has
not been easy. Nor has it been entirely successful, at least not at the
foundational or creedal level.

In 1965, as the Second Vatican Council was winding to its con-
clusion, Patriarch Athenagoras I of the Eastern or Greek Church
and Pope Paul VI of the Western or Latin Church met together in
a gesture of goodwill and absolute intention. Each of them brought
to that meeting a thousand years of history in which the various
predecessors of each had formally and several times over excommunicated from the Body of Christ on earth and/or anathematized the
predecessors of the other. In the course of their meeting, the patriarch

and the pope formally lifted those millennium-old anathemas and excommunications. It was a monumental step that would have been inconceivable only a half century or so before.

In that same year of 1965, the North American Orthodox-Catholic Theological Consultation was founded. As its name would indicate, the Consultation was, like the meeting of the primates, a deliberated and official attempt to arrive at a rapprochement of sorts between the Eastern and the Western Churches. That effort has borne, if not a bumper crop, then at least a modicum of fruit. In 1989, in an event that sent shockwaves through the media, if not through the Church per se, Pope John Paul II and Patriarch Demetrius knelt together in Rome and recited the Nicene Creed without the *filioque*. There have now been a total of three subsequent occasions when the leaders of East and West have done likewise. Additionally, several ecumenical commissions of Orthodox and Catholic theologians have agreed since then that in their work together, they will step back from even engaging this old dividing point.

Despite the fact that popes and patriarchs have jointly knelt to pray the creed without the *filioque*, however, the deeply religious of the East and West still remain profoundly divided and suspicious of each other. Indeed, one would have a very difficult time finding an Eastern bishop today who is not very conscious of the fact that the recent Roman pope was, before gaining his tiara, Cardinal Ratzinger and that it was Cardinal Ratzinger who is on record as having referred to all Eastern churches as "static" and "petrified as it were."[6]

Perhaps less inflammatory and more studied, not to mention more useful, are the opening paragraphs of *The Filioque: A Church Dividing Issue? An Agreed Statement*, issued in October 2003 by the North American Orthodox-Catholic Theological Consultation. Those opening sentences read in part:

From 1999 until 2003, the North American Orthodox-Catholic Consultation has focused its discussions on an issue that has been identified, for more than twelve centuries, as one of the root causes of division between our Churches: our divergent ways of conceiving and speaking about the origin of the Holy Spirit within the inner life of the triune God. . . . [T]he presence of this term (*filioque*) in the Western version of the Creed has been a source of scandal for Eastern Christians, both because of the Trinitarian theology it expresses, and because it had been adopted by a growing number of Churches in the West into the canonical formulation of a received ecumenical council without corresponding ecumenical agreement.[7]

In other words, schisms matter. They also heal only imperfectly, as a rule.

Notes

1. To more fully appreciate the actual naivete of the bishops' position, one should consult A. Edward Siecienski's *The Filioque: History of a Doctrinal Controversy*, in which he argues authoritatively that the bishops in Toledo had "no consciousness that they were introducing something novel" (New York: Oxford University Press, 2010), 69.

2. More than we could ever manage to comprehend today, liturgical practice was everything a thousand years ago. Spoken words had power, and that power led all too often, as in this case, to unbelievably bloody conflict.

3. Lest we be accused of a certain cynicism in our treatment of Henry, we must add here that he became one of the most effective emperors in Western history. His defeat of Gregory's attempt to seize the papacy and his restoration of Benedict to it were interpreted in his own lifetime as having saved the Church. A century later, he was canonized in recognition of that fact, as was his wife, Cunigunde, shortly thereafter.

4. A little more than a century ago, sociologist Max Weber called this sort of confluence of disintegration "the disenchantment of the world." There probably never has been, and never shall be, a more poignant or more accurate naming than that.

5. There could probably not be a better or more auspicious time than ours, in fact, for us to reflect on what happened then and what it means for us now. In doing so, we would do well to consider the words of one of the twentieth

century's great Orthodox theologians on the impact of the *filioque*, purely as a theological idea:

> In Latin theology, the divine Persons were considered as the simple inner relations of the unique essence of the Godhead: hence, if the very existence of the Spirit is determined by its relations to the Father and the Son, the doctrine of the *Filioque*—or procession of the Spirit from the Father and the Son—becomes a logical, dogmatic necessity, for the Spirit cannot be said to be distinct from the Son if he does not proceed from him. Eastern theologians, on the other hand, remained faithful to the old "personalism" of the Greek Fathers. The doctrine of the *Filioque* appeared to them, consequently, as Semi-Sabellianism (to use the expression of Photius). . . . Consubstantial with the Father and the Son, because proceeding from the Father, the unique source of the Deity, the Spirit has his own existence and personal function in the inner life of God and the economy of salvation: his task is to bring about the unity of the human race in the Body of Christ, but he also imparts to this unity a personal, and hence diversified, character. It is with a prayer to the Holy Spirit that all the liturgical services of the Orthodox Church begin, and with an invocation of his name that the eucharistic mystery is effected. (John Meyendorff, *The Orthodox Church: Its Past and Its Role in the World Today* [Crestwood, NY: St. Vladimir's Seminary Press, 1981], 196–97)

6. Cardinal Ratzinger made his caustic remarks in 1985 in *The Ratzinger Report*, a series of interviews the cardinal gave to an Italian reporter but that nevertheless read today like a Catholic Wikileaks.

7. The reader who wishes may see more of this seminal document which was, last we checked, at http://www.usccb.org/beliefs-and-teachings/ecumenical-and-interreligious/ecumenical/orthodox/filioque-church-dividing-issue-english.cfm.

Prayer Offered before the Opening of Each Session of the Second Vatican Council, 1962–65

We stand before you, Holy Spirit,
conscious of our sinfulness,
but aware that we gather in your name.

Come to us, remain with us,
and enlighten our hearts.

Give us light and strength
to know your will,
to make it our own,
and to live it in our lives.

Guide us by your wisdom,
support us by your power,
for you are God, sharing the glory of Father and Son.

You desire justice for all;
enable us to uphold the rights of others;

do not allow us to be misled by ignorance
or corrupted by fear or favor.

Unite us to yourself in the bond of love
and keep us faithful to all that is true.

As we gather in your name, may we temper justice
   with love,
so that all our discussions and reflections
may be pleasing to you, and earn the reward
promised to good and faithful servants.

We ask this of You who live and reign with the
Father and the Son, one God, for ever and ever.
   Amen.

PART 2

Matters
of the SPIRIT

9

Credo

A Most Dangerous Word

For most of the first two millennia of latinized Christianity, rightly knowing and rightly confessing one's positions on issues of Christian faith and Christian doctrine were, quite literally, matters of life and death. Today most of us have left the horrors of such times behind us. Primarily we have managed to do that because, in large part, we have left behind us those forms of cultural and political organization that require religious authority and a certain unity of religious opinion in order to maintain the civil stability necessary for their survival.

Admittedly, there are still today some few areas of the latinized world where doctrinal rectitude is more or less socially and politically mandatory. Even given that fact, though, few of us fear for our physical lives should we get some of the details wrong or, even worse, should we willfully adapt some of them to accommodate private or idiosyncratic credos.[1]

This shift to less violent—and considerably less fatal—ways obviously constitutes a marked improvement in human affairs. Apparently, however, it can no more free many of us from a kind of endemic, historic, ongoing absorption with "getting it right" than it can unsay the horrors of our history. The informing problem with this particular monomaniacal absorption is, of course, that there are almost as many "correct" arrangements of the finer points as there are distinct groupings within Christianity.

The very existence of denominations in the Protestantism born out of the Great Reformation bears stout and ongoing testimony to a Christian fascination with doctrinal particularities. Correctly parsing the Scriptures and intellectually resolving in a satisfying manner the apparent paradoxes in them, determining by precedent the acceptable levels of sacramental and liturgical practice, extrapolating and consecrating modes of personal conduct as requisite to divine acceptance—all of them are admittedly still the preoccupation of contemporary Protestantism as well as much of the *raison d'etre* for its many, many parts.[2] Certainly there is no question, however, about the fact that the exquisitely hierarchal communions of the Roman Catholicism and Orthodoxy that preceded Protestantism were, and still are, pathologically preoccupied with doctrinal correctness just as surely as their methods of arriving at resolution were, and still are, superficially at least, far less egalitarian.

Thus it was that, by the eleventh century, confession had come to be a bloody and deadly serious business, which is where we left our tale in part 1.

In the centuries following Rome's conquest of Greece in the second century BCE, the East and the West had done business together out of enforced necessity. At times they had cohabited with varying degrees of mutual affection just as both had, at other times, exercised outright cultural animosity one toward the other. Most of the time through the centuries, the accommodation between the two had been simply an uneasy but accepted fact of life. It was, nonetheless, almost inevitable that at some future point an irreparable rupture would occur. All that would be required was for either Rome or Byzantium (in due time, Constantinople, of course) to have a head of state powerful enough and aggrieved enough to risk the potential dangers of secession and severance. That happened in 1054 CE.

The Great Schism of 1054 CE, when it finally did come, was obviously the final rending asunder of a cultural divide that had been festering for over a millennium. The *filioque* only provided doctrinal cover for a whole catalog of intensely felt cultural, spiritual, and political differences that had become too ubiquitous and too intrusive to be ignored any longer. The arts and philosophy and language of Hellenism and the more utilitarian attributes of Western culture had been caught for far too long in deadly gridlock, and only a question of the magnitude of the who, what, and how of the Holy Spirit seemed worthy of so great an arbitration as the times required.

Credo alone was not sufficient; it must become *Credemus*.

Notes

1. The general tendency in Emergence Christian theology is to question with real vigor and precision whether or not the connection between faith and doctrinal precision is essential to the soul's salvation. Dogma, yes, but doctrine, not so much. That is, do one's brainwaves and verbal utterances actually make one's faith? Emergence Christians can often take this even a step further and reference those places of spiritual primacy where Jesus taught (as in his judgment of the nations as told in the Gospel of Matthew, for example) that a life is what constitutes and demonstrates a disciple, rather than a mind-set. Confession, in other words, has ceased to be so vital, and therefore, such a bloody battlefield.

All that having been said, though, one certainly can still find in Emergence Christianity some defining tensions among and between its member parts. Emerging Christians are not nearly as gender-inclusive as are Emergent Christians, for example; but then of course, neither Emergents nor Neo-monastics nor Hyphenateds are as homophobic as Emergings, either. Points of differentiation still exist, in other words; there still are metaphorical boxes to tick off and invisible lines not to be crossed. But there are also far fewer doctrines to be confessed than once there were and, by the grace of God and the ages, *Credo—I believe*—really is a far less danger-fraught word with which to begin a sentence.

2. A list of such discrete and distinguishable units, in and of itself, now approaches thirty-seven thousand worldwide by even the most conservative estimates.

10

Breath, Bread, and Beards

One of the central and more fundamental of the differences between West and East was what we today might simply call a variance of the imagination. We have already seen several examples of how the Greek mind and language differ from that of the latinized West. One of those, in particular, is worthy of being re-mentioned just here.

The Hebrew word *ruach* (meaning both "breath" and "spirit"), which occurs throughout the Hebrew Scriptures for *God*, was translated into the Greek of the New Testament as *pneuma*, which also means "breath" and sometimes "spirit" or sometimes as *hagion pneuma*, "holy breath" or "holy spirit." Greek Christians, as a result, speaking the very language of the New Testament throughout the ages, knew and have known God not as the "Holy Spirit" of Latin (and later of Germanic) construction, but quite literally, as the "Holy Breath." How much easier it was, then, for the Greek imagination to grasp the third person of the Trinity as distinct from and indistinguishable from the other two than it was—or ever would be—for the Western imagination! This "breath" is the person of the One who gives to all living things their life, their breath.

One of the more telling characteristics of Emergence Christianity in almost all of its components is a growing rapprochement with—or perhaps, better said, an increasingly sympathetic affinity for—portions of the theology and praxis of both Judaism and Orthodoxy. Predictably enough, then, this non-Western and/or Jewish way of conceiving of or perceiving the Holy Spirit as breath has deep resonance for many Emergence Christians. Seen from that point of view, the nuances of the metaphor are most beautifully and perhaps most accessibly articulated in one of the footnotes in the *siddur*, or prayer book, of the Reconstructionist movement within contemporary Judaism. There a commentator reflects on how three words in Hebrew, *nefesh*, *ruach*, and *neshamah*, often translate as "soul" or "spirit" and yet also mean "human breath":

> Breath is the prerequisite of life and speech, of existence and communication, and it is a gift requiring no conscious attention except in cases of illness. If each inhalation required a direct order, each exhalation a conscious command, how should we find energy or attention for anything else? How should we sleep? In truth, we do not breathe; we are breathed.[1]

Be all of that as it may, the truth still is that our worlds are defined by our language and that our worlds are only as conceivable to others as the words that we are able to give to our imaginings. What sort of world did *filioque* in its day create—or reflect—for the Greek mind? What for that of the Roman? We will never know, of course, for we cannot even imagine what we cannot imagine how to speak aloud.

Well beyond the very foundational limitation of the power of the human imagination to expand and restrict the scope of operative truth, there were, and still are, other points of difference, of course, between the two great cultures of the Mediterranean world. While those differences of theology and praxis are too numerous to name here and while not all of them are even germane to our discussion, a brief look at two or three of them might be of help in understanding the fierceness and animosity of the Great Schism.

Rome or Constantinople? That, ultimately, was the Great Question. The church began in Jerusalem in Jesus's day and was led, after his resurrection, by the ethnically and religiously Jewish; but soon thereafter it would find its locus in the Rome of St. Paul, of St. Peter, and of the other early martyrs who gave their lives to the faith there in that place. The Church was built upon the blood of the martyrs—built upon blood shed in Rome. Thus, Rome would continue for centuries, and even to this day, to consider herself the locus of universal Christianity, based on her historical primacy.

But with the coming of Constantine as emperor in the fourth century, what was the epicenter of the universe was no longer always Rome. The epicenter, from time to time and increasingly, would be in Constantinople. And ultimately, of course, it was Constantinople that became the primary seat of the new Byzantine Empire. Thus began the West-East tug that would lead—albeit gradually and circuitously—to secession and separation and schism.

In time, the bishop of Rome came to be not a mere bishop but the pope and, by his own assertion, the spiritual and ecclesial leader of "true" Christianity. By the same kind of alienating process, the "true" spiritual leader of the East became the ecumenical patriarch, at least in his mind and that of the eastern end of the Mediterranean and those countries adjacent to it. Those two opposing positions and their succession of intractable primates would do much of their developing separately and independently from the fourth century onwards, the West continuing to hold to its authority *de jure* (rather than *de facto*), and the East eschewing the notion of a church organized on a single, universal plane.[2]

Latin or Greek? This was a far trickier question. At least it was a trickier one than might, at first blush, seem to have been the case. After the Aramaic-speaking, Hebrew-speaking Jewish-Christians of the first generation of Jesus-followers were dead, the next two centuries of Christians shared one language: Greek.[3] But almost unconsciously and without premeditation, in the decades before First Nicaea (325 CE), Christians in the West began increasingly to employ the more familiar Latin of their public affairs for conveying their ecclesiastical ones. As a result, the influence and nuances and subtleties of Greek would continue to be dominant in the East, though they had begun their slow fade in the West.

So it is that to this day, the legacy of the classical era of Western civilization is Greek (or "Hellenic," and later, "Byzantine") east of the Adriatic Sea, and Latin to the west of it. The language of philosophy, sculpture, athletics, educational theory, religion and mythology, and literature was born in the Greek East, while the Latin of St. Jerome's Vulgate Bible would come to dominate in the West. Greeks were understandably proud of their rich heritage of history and mythology and of themselves as the people who gave birth to philosophy, the queen of the sciences. Their Latin counterparts in the West emphasized instead their political prowess, empire, and worldwide reach, in opposition to such ethereal and headier pursuits. These distinctions still play out again and again in our own day as, whether consciously or not and almost by gut-level instinct, the West values most unity and strength among Christians while the East grants overarching and prime value to tradition and reason.

The ultimate truth in all of this, though, is that no theological dispute is ever about theology alone. Most certainly, the Great Schism was not just about the *filioque*. Just as surely, of course, the *filioque* was not the sum total of all there was to know about the nature and Christian understanding of Holy Trinity.

Notes

1. Everett Gendler, *Kol Haneshamah: Shabbat Vehagim*, 3rd ed. (Wyncote, PA: The Reconstructionist Press, 1996), 235.

2. Yves Congar, *After Nine Hundred Years: The Background of the Schism between the Eastern and Western Churches* (New York: Fordham University Press, 1959), 13.

3. Henry Chadwick, *East and West: The Making of a Rift in the Church* (New York: Oxford University Press, 2005), 8.

11

An Act of Moral Fratricide

As things turned out, and as we know, centuries of forced commonality and endured differences came to their breaking point at last in the eleventh century. And because the power brokers who held hegemony and exercised governance both in Rome and in Constantinople were ecclesial rather than hereditary rulers, that breaking point found its expression not in a military confrontation but in a confessional split. Where once there had been one confession, now there were two, and they differed from one another over a phrase that would, by secular standards, seem surprisingly innocuous: *filioque*.

In Toledo in 589 CE, when the *filioque* had first been added to the Creed, the means—or unilateral method, if one prefers that harsher term—used for its insertion had exposed what was to become, over the subsequent four hundred plus years, the true basis for disagreement between the churches of the East and the West. Doctrinally, the two communions had scrimmaged for almost half a millennium—just as they have continued to scrimmage ever since—over the nature of the Holy Spirit without arriving at mutual agreement or resolution. There is no question about that. But the unpardonable error was not so much doctrinal as ecclesial: The insertion of the *filioque* had assumed the right of a single person to represent Christ on earth.

Toledo in 589 CE had set aside the wisdom of councils—had demeaned and denied the very wisdom of the first apostles who established the councils as the Church's proper means of discernment and governance—and it had dared to replace conciliar wisdom with little more than the arbitrary perspective of one man and/or of one region.

The East could never accept such a position. It was as if the West were saying: "We no longer call you our ecclesiastical equals. We are no longer brothers." So bitter and deep was the offense that writing almost a millennium later, Alexei Khomiakov, a Russian religious writer of the early nineteenth century, aptly called it an act of "moral fratricide."[1] It was.

Which is why, in 1054, the bishops of the East would finally come to employ language that was, and remains, anything but cool and detached:

> We do not wish to tamper with the sacred and holy creed, which holds its authority inviolate from synodal and ecumenical decrees, by the use of wrongful arguments, illegal reasoning, and extreme boldness. And unlike them, we do not wish to say that the Holy Spirit proceeds from the Father and the Son—O what artifice of the devil![2]

While moral fratricide was most certainly neither the intention nor the anticipated result behind the insertion of the *filioque* in sixth-century Spain, it not only infuriated Byzantine Christians but also almost immediately re-opened discussions about what it means to worship only one God. Nor is it a matter of coincidence that, shortly after Toledo, Eastern leaders began to speak of another possibility—one that was less theological and quite definitely ecclesial.

Subtly at first, perhaps even coyly, if churchmen may be said to be coy, those Eastern leaders spoke of another possibility. Then, in time, they gave up subtlety and began, instead, to speak quite openly of the historical probability that St. Peter had founded the see of Antioch as well as that of Rome, and that—let the ages beware!—in fact Antioch held ecclesiastical precedence over Rome. Rome, after all, was that distant city where the pope resided and from which all evil had always come since the days of the early apostles and the very founding of the Church herself.

The insults back and forth were as deeply personal as any label of moral fratricide could ever suggest. They were so personal, in fact, that few observers on either side of the argument have ever been foolish enough to even try to argue that the Great Schism occurred primarily because of a difference of lofty ideas about the proper understanding of Trinitarian God. Fine and lofty ideas about God accounted for only a fraction of what actually was happening between Constantinople and Rome in those torturous days. This was about power, both ecclesiastical and civil, and it was about a cultural and spiritual gap that had never been bridged despite many valiant attempts. The Great Schism revealed—and then deepened—far more wide-ranging political, economic, social, and ecclesiastical implications than it ever did doctrinal ones.

The mutual anathemas in 1054 between Cardinal Humbert, acting as emissary of Pope Leo IX, and Patriarch Michael Cerularius were just the beginning—and not at all surprising. By every account, Cardinal Humbert and Patriarch Michael Cerularius were mirror images of each other: they were each partisan, caustic, "intolerant and overbearing," and pugilistic.[3] These were not diplomatic men, nor were they like the conciliatory ecumenical officers we in our time have come to know over the last century. No, they were fighters.

The events of the first several months of 1054 moved quickly. In January, Leo IX sent a letter to Patriarch Michael declaring that the Holy See in Rome was the true and only office for ruling the universal Christian Church. He based his opinion on the Donation of Constantine, a document soon thereafter proven to be a forgery (but probably sincerely believed to be legitimate by Leo).

In April, a delegation from Leo IX and led by Cardinal Humbert arrived in Constantinople to discuss all these and other matters of contention—and there were so many by this point that one wonders what the delegation was actually intending to do. The Italian emissaries were, nevertheless, received with honor. Yet even as the Romans were in the process of being received by the patriarch, the pope himself died in Rome (April 19). Moreover—and perhaps more immediately consequential—the seal of a letter from Leo to Patriarch Michael was discovered to have been tampered with and, as an obvious result, was distrusted by the Byzantines. What was already a highly charged political situation soon began to boil ever more rapidly.

It was a hot summer day on July 16, 1054, when Cardinal Humbert and his various attendants made their way from the Latin quarter of Constantinople toward Hagia Sophia. The great cathedral—the largest in all of Christendom—was at that moment filled to the brim with worshippers. The Divine Liturgy was about to begin, Matins having just ended. The announcement at the beginning of the service— "Blessed is the Kingdom of the Father and of the Son and of the Holy Spirit, now and forever, and to the ages of ages"—was about to be proclaimed to all who had gathered. Humbert knew precisely what he was doing. The cardinal walked boldly into the church at that moment, stepping into that gorgeous, cavernous nave below its sculpted, scalloped, shell dome, striding his way up to the altar. There, he laid a parchment firmly down with a slap.

This was a bull of excommunication placed upon Patriarch Michael and other Eastern leaders, and a demand that they accept the Roman pope as their superior if they ever wanted to be welcomed back into Christ's kingdom. It was a bull that, by the way, could no longer be deemed valid since the pope in whose name it was written was dead, and Leo's successor would not ascend the chair of St. Peter until April of the following year. Rome, in other words, was, at least for the time being, without a pope.

Undeterred by all of this, Cardinal Humbert, standing in Hagia Sophia, began to denigrate the Eastern Church's leader by referring to Michael as a "false neophyte patriarch," among other distasteful and sundry things, and accusing him of "extremely wicked crimes" including—ah, herein lieth the rub—having "deleted from the creed the procession of the Holy Spirit from the Son"![4]

Having said his piece, Humbert made his way out of Hagia Sophia. Then stopping just outside its massive doors and with the appropriate dramatic pause, he quite literally shook the dust of the cathedral from his feet. Didn't the great Gospel writer say, after all: "If anyone will not welcome you or listen to your words, shake off the dust from your feet as you leave that house or town. Truly I tell you, it will be more tolerable for the land of Sodom and Gomorrah on the day of judgment than for that town" (Matt. 10:14–15)?

The perspective of Eastern leaders, after the shock had worn off and their Divine Liturgy had been concluded, was how pretentious their cousins suddenly seemed to be. And evil. A few of the more benevolent Eastern leaders began to imagine that their Western counterparts could not possibly be so arrogant and disrespectful as their strange cardinal had been. Something else must be going on.

Peter III of Antioch, for example, hypothesized that the Latins, after being conquered by the Vandals and held under their sway for so long, must have simply misplaced all of their original documents from First Nicaea. Perhaps that would explain their actions. Of course, he also believed—and instructed others to understand—that the Latins were naturally of a more barbaric race and that that should not be held too much against them. "From rusticity or ignorance they often lapse from what is right," he said.[5] Evil. Barbarian. Ignorant. The Greeks would begin to use these three words more and more often, time and again, to try to understand what their Latin counterparts had done.

Then on July 24th, eight days later, after Cardinal Humbert's dramatic shaking of Orthodox dust off his Roman feet, Patriarch Michael countered his gesture. The patriarch ceremonially burned the bull left by the cardinal and his papal delegation. After that, there was no turning back. Anathemas were spit back and forth from East to West, and additional excommunications followed, like carrier pigeons, from West to East. Each side knew that God wanted to condemn the other and all of their followers to eternal damnation, or worse. What had been snowballing since long before 1014 reached its culmination in 1054 and now rested like a giant, arctic freeze over the Bosphorus Strait.

For a brief time, between about 1070 and 1080, there seemed a possibility of reunion. Between a new emperor, Michael (VII Ducas), and a new pope, Gregory VII, there was for a time "the prospect of ecclesiastical rapprochement and the establishment in the East of the new papalism," but that moment was brief, and the East, so to speak, came to its senses.[6]

Still, in 1095, Pope Urban II called for Norman crusaders to travel to Constantinople to join "their Byzantine brethren" to fight for the Holy Land. In part, Urban acted in response to the request of Byzantine Emperor Alexius I, who was being besieged by Muslim

Turks on his borders; but he also acted in the hope that a joint cause would become healing for West and East alike. It wasn't to be, however.[7] Even on the battlefields, the two sides and the soldiers who composed them were bickering among themselves so much that they seemed no longer to be co-religionists. Each side began to recognize the other's baptisms as invalid. Then each questioned the sacraments of the other's altar. Then, in time, the insults turned to true atrocities.

Less than ninety years later, in May 1182, religious violence seized the region and what is known now as the Massacre of the Latins began. The Latin quarter of Constantinople was a residential and commercial holdover of sorts from the First Crusade and home to some fifty-plus thousand Latin Catholics, almost all of whom were murdered that month at the hands of the Greek-speaking majority in the city. With thousands dead in the streets and in their own homes, the few remaining thousand were sold into slavery to the Turks.[8] Three years after that, in 1185, in gross retaliation, Latins attacked Thessalonica, one of the great Greek cities, also killing indiscriminately and this time, even raping the nuns.

Less than twenty years later, with Muslims once again in control of Jerusalem and most of the Holy Land, the Normans set out across Western and then Eastern Europe for the Holy Land. But what began as another attempt to free the holiest places of Christendom for pilgrimage and commerce first detoured and then degenerated into a near-complete rape and devastation of Byzantine Christendom. One prominent Western cleric, who later became the abbot of St. Denis, even remarked that, due to the East's rejection of the *filioque*, as well as other differences of doctrine and practice, "the Greeks had incurred the hatred of our men, for their error had become known even among the lay people. Because of this they were judged not to be Christians, and the Franks considered killing them a matter of no importance and hence could with the more difficulty be restrained from pillaging and plundering."[9]

In the course of the Fourth Crusade (1202–4), the West effectively nailed down the coffin on any hope of a united church by conquering and occupying Constantinople and by forcing the authority of the West down Eastern throats. The Western knights sacked Constantinople, plundering and willfully destroying those whom, not so long before, they had considered as fellow Christians. "A *filioque* in your creed, or the sword," the Easterners were told. The Latins believed their actions to be biblical—an eye for an eye—while the Greeks viewed their former cousins as "forerunners of the Anti-Christ, the agents and harbingers of his anticipated ungodliness."[10]

Only the wars between Catholics and Protestants in England in the seventeenth century or today's constant threat of religious violence in Kashmir, between a Muslim Pakistan and a Hindu India, can compare to the magnificent scope and religious passion of this most dreadful century and a half of woe.

Notes

1. Quoted in A. Edward Siecienski, *The Filioque: History of a Doctrinal Controversy* (New York: Oxford University Press, 2010), 3.

2. Deno John Geanakoplos, *Byzantium: Church, Society, and Civilization Seen through Contemporary Eyes* (Chicago: University of Chicago Press, 1984), 209.

3. J. M. Hussey, *The Orthodox Church in the Byzantine Empire* (Oxford: Clarendon Press, 1986), 133.

4. It is important to remember that Pope Leo IX died in April 1054, two months before his cardinal actually excommunicated the Eastern patriarch. Many scholars believe that it was mostly Humbert's doing, not the pope's, but we shall never know for sure. Also, today, in a telling bit of historical irony, Hagia Sophia has been completely secularized by the Turkish government. After centuries of religious coups—from Orthodox to Catholic to Muslim mosque—God-worship is completely forbidden. Hagia Sophia is, today, a museum.

5. Quoted in Siecienski, *The Filioque*, 116.

6. Aristeides Papadakis, *The Christian East and the Rise of the Papacy: The Church AD 1071–1453* (Crestwood, NY: St. Vladimir's Seminary Press, 1994), 75.

7. See Carl Erdmann, *The Origin of the Idea of Crusade*, trans. Marshall W. Baldwin and Walter Goffart (Princeton: Princeton University Press, 1977), 349–50. And the more recent *The First Crusade: The Call from the East*, by Peter Frankopan (Cambridge, MA: Harvard University Press, 2012).

8. Donald M. Nicol, *Byzantium and Venice: A Study in Diplomatic and Cultural Relations* (New York: Cambridge University Press, 1992), 107. As Robert Browning once wrote: "The curious crime, the fine / Felicity and flower of wickedness" (*The Ring and the Book*, Book X).

9. Odo of Deuil, as quoted in Papadakis, *Christian East*, 103. Additionally, as we have indicated in the body of this discussion, there were indeed some very serious and fiercely argued ecclesial differences between the Greek and the Latin churches in addition to the theological one of the *filioque*. A brief summary of some of them may be found in Appendix C.

10. Nicetas Choniates, *The Sack of Constantinople*, trans. D. C. Munro (Philadelphia: University of Pennsylvania Press, 1912), 16. Long after these events, if you fast-forward to 1870, you will see the Latin Roman Church declaring papal infallibility. Game over.

12

Joachim of Fiore and the Dawning of a New Age

If this were a novel, we would introduce you now to a new character. We would tell you about a singular man born less than a century after the Great Schism, in 1135 CE, in Calabria, the Italian "toe" region that lies at the end of the peninsula and is surrounded by the Ionian and Tyrrhenian seas. This is not a novel, of course, but as it happens, this twelfth-century monk is essential to the story we're telling. And strangely enough, if you want to begin to understand how the Great Schism, *filioque*, and the Spirit of God all have come to matter so much to us in the last century, you have to look back nearly a thousand years at the enigmatic Joachim of Fiore.

His Italian mother named him Gioacchino, but history has anglicized him to Joachim. He began adult life as a court clerk and notary, appointed to high-placed officials, including the archbishop of Palermo. A bureaucrat, he was nevertheless religiously active and spiritually sensitive, and while on a pilgrimage to Jerusalem as a twenty-four-year-old, he felt God stirring his soul.

Soon after his return from the Holy Land, young Joachim left career and family behind for the monastic life. Then he intensified his commitment to seek God by becoming a hermit, and relatively soon after that he was called back from "the desert" in order to become an abbot leading other monks. Eventually he founded a monastic order in Fiore, in his native southern Italian hills, and as a result, he's forever since been known as Joachim of Fiore.

Joachim was a student of the Scriptures in a time when the Bible was still believed to contain deep and opaque mysteries—to be, in effect, a rich allegory whose truths were hidden well beneath its surface. Behind every phrase and verse there were subtle understandings ready to elude simple minds, and it was in this context that Joachim began his life's work of interpreting Scripture allegorically, constantly finding in it meanings that were spiritually measured and spiritually defined. Joachim was not unusual in teaching the Bible this way, of course, but the particular genius that he brought to the work and the way in which his conclusions resonated with the feelings of the people of his era made him stand out.

Joachim had a mind for facts and details, but he was also the creator of meta-theories. As such, he became a fierce critic of one of the most popular theological ideas of his age, famously posited by Peter Lombard in a work entitled *Four Books of Sentences. Four Books* was actually one book—a medieval textbook, in fact—that was studied by every serious student of theology. In it, Lombard taught that the Godhead, in the purest and most ideal sense, could never possibly be known in this world. God could be contemplated but never truly understood.

In all fairness, Joachim probably believed that Lombard was a Sabellianist, that is, that he was a member of an openly heretical school of thought that was willing to trade in the essential threeness of God for the sake of a high version of the unity of the Godhead. Regardless of whether that justification is true or not, Joachim disagreed vehemently with the *Sentences*, insisting that God, in fact, wants to be known in history and in the workings of the world in each era. It was that battle of ideas that paved the way for the coming of Joachim's most important meta-theory of all.

Because of his engagement with Lombard, Joachim came to a point in his own biblical and historical work where he believed that he could see all of human history divided into three epochs or dispensations. He, in fact, believed that God had revealed this personally to him. As a result, his most important teaching—which he preached and wrote about in many places throughout his life—became that the world is moving through these three successive eras or epochs and that these eras mirror the economy of the Holy Trinity itself. He taught that there was an Age of the Father, now past, an Age of the Son, still present, and an Age of the Spirit, emerging.

This was not unprecedented. The church fathers and mothers, for instance, had long explained that the persons of the Trinity were gradually revealed by the Godhead for a reason. These are the words of one of the great Eastern "doctors" of the church, Gregory of Nazianzus:

The old covenant made clear proclamation of the Father, a less definite one of the Son. The new covenant made the Son manifest and gave us a glimpse of the Spirit's Godhead. At the present time, the Spirit resides amongst us, giving us a clearer manifestation of himself than before. It was dangerous for the Son to be preached openly when the Godhead of the Father was still unacknowledged. It was dangerous, too, for the Holy Spirit to be made (and here I use a rather rash expression) an extra burden, when the Son had not been received. . . . No, God meant it to be by piecemeal additions, "ascents" as David called them, by progress and advance from glory to glory, that the light of the Trinity should shine upon more illustrious souls.[1]

Joachim became a serious student of these "piecemeal additions," so-called. In an elaborate series of biblical commentaries and theological treaties—he wrote so many that he had had to dictate them to various scribes and disciples—he determined that the very structure of the world, its history, and God's way of working in it would move through these three stages:

- The world had seen the Age of the Father, which Joachim identified with the Old Testament: its teachings, its ways of understanding God, and God's ways of interacting with the creation. In the words of Joachim, this first period was a time when human beings were like "slaves," an era "ascribed to the Father, who is the author of all things."[2] The first era concluded at the time of Christ.

- Then came the Age of the Son, born in the era of the New Testament, and marked by the birth of God in human form and the growth of the church. Christ is he "who has been esteemed worthy to share our mud."[3] This was the era of human beings as "sons" not "slaves," and was waning, Joachim said, in his own day.

- Emerging, then, was the Age of the Spirit, dawning soon, he wrote, and a time when humankind would relate primarily to the third member of the Trinity. This would be a moment marked by a decreased importance in ecclesial structures, sacraments, creeds, and clergy, when all people would begin to relate more directly "as friends" to the Divine. Joachim saw the seed of this idea in the imagination of St. Paul, quoting 2 Corinthians 3:17, "Now the Lord is the Spirit, and where the Spirit of the Lord is, there is freedom."

Joachim was also a visual thinker, if ever the world has seen one, and he often used visual tricks and tools to aid his own memory and that of others. Three of them are relevant here. In the first, using the upper case of the *alpha*, or first letter, of the Greek alphabet, Joachim imagined the Holy Spirit as equal to the Son before the Father. God the Father is symbolized as the top of the *alpha*, processing downward on one arm to the Son, and on the other to the Spirit, yet with all three connected, one to the other and each necessary to the completeness of the construct.

In the second piece of pairing, the third member of the Trinity takes a position of real prominence and power. Using the lower case of *omega*, the last letter of the Greek alphabet, Joachim taught that the left arm of the *omega* is the *Pater*, the right arm is the *Filius*, and the center where the two come together is the *Spiritus Sanctus*.[4]

Alpha (upper case)   Omega (lower case)

And perhaps most familiar to us today, Joachim's preoccupation with the circularity and interrelatedness of the Trinity led to the popularization of the so-called Borromean rings as the accepted visual symbol of the Trinity.

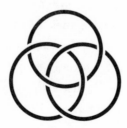

The work of the Holy Spirit, Joachim believed, was to be the culmination of history. It was to usher in the final, glorious time beyond all time called eternity. But this was not your typical apocalyptic prediction. Joachim was not looking for the end of the world. He was instead seeking its final and culminating era. This is where he was unique: Joachim was studying the meaning of God, looking at the trajectory of human history, and identifying a new day of openness, inspiration, and intimacy between God and earth. Although he never used the now-popular phrase, Joachim was perhaps the first to foresee our own new era of "horizontal transcendence."

Joachim, however, was also nothing if not complex. He occasionally contradicted himself, and he used every numeric symbol he could. Beyond that, world events did not always fit neatly into three successive eras. In fact, Joachim also, and perhaps as a bow to tradition, taught the two traditional, more generally understood covenants:

- The Old: from the creation of the world until the advent of the Son.
- The New: from that advent, the Incarnation, until the Second Coming.

The Old was, within Joachim's taxonomy, the Age of the Father. The New was the Age of the Son. Then, as the consummation of all things previously accomplished, would come the blessed time beyond time when the person of the Spirit—in a triumphant sort of reversal and reinterpretation of the diminishing effect that the *filioque* had performed on the Godhead—completes everything. The Spirit who hovered over the waters of first-created matter and who appeared as a sign when the incarnate One came out of John's baptismal waters would now hover, again, and in that hovering somehow illuminate, accompany, and move us closer than ever toward the heavenly kingdom.

Those are the essential ideas of Joachim of Fiore,[5] and one cannot help but acknowledge that by means of them he initiated a conversation that is as active among us today as it was among both his own contemporaries and also among those who followed over the following centuries.

Is our era the one that Joachim foresaw? Is the upheaval of the present moment, of this every-five-hundred-year shakeup in the church, the sign that the Age of the Spirit is upon us? Who knows? Many a well-trained and credentialed theologian has considered the question over the last few decades, certainly, and one of the most credentialed and respected of them, Bernard McGinn, professor emeritus of historical theology and the history of Christianity at the Divinity School of the University of Chicago was very clear recently on PBS's *Frontline* about his assessment of Joachim:

> Joachim of Fiore is the most important apocalyptic thinker of the whole medieval period, and maybe after the prophet John, the most important apocalyptic thinker in the history of Christianity.[6]

In any event, though, the old Chinese proverb/curse still says, "May you live in interesting times," and this is how Joachim presented the portent of a true Age of the Spirit. The Spirit is unsettled, not settled, wild, not tame. As Joachim would say and as the Gospel of John puts it, quoting Jesus: "Do not be astonished that I said to you, 'You must be born from above.' The wind blows where it chooses, and you hear the sound of it, but you do not know where it comes from or where it goes. So it is with everyone who is born of the Spirit" (John 3:7–8).

Notes

1. Gregory of Nazianzus, "The Fifth Theological Oration: On the Holy Spirit," in *On God and Christ* (Crestwood, NY: St. Vladimir's Seminary Press, 2002), orat. 31.26, p. 137.

2. Quotes from Joachim of Fiore in this section are the translations of Gianni Vattimo, *After Christianity*, Italian Academy Lectures, trans. Luca D'Isanto (New York: Columbia University Press, 2002), 30.

3. Vattimo and D'Isanto, *After Christianity*, 30.

4. Marjorie Reeves, *Joachim of Fiore and the Prophetic Future* (New York: Harper, 1977), 6–8.

5. Regrettably, our brief coverage here can give scarcely more than the slightest suggestion of Joachim's scope and certainly of his influence. Dante, for example, was a great admirer of Joachim's work and, in *The Divine Comedy*, placed him in Paradise. According to some sources, Richard the Lionhearted stopped on his way to the Third Crusade in order to be taught by Joachim. Even as recently as 2008, there was a spurious but energetic inundation of chitchat about the fact that Barack Obama had quoted Joachim three times in his preelection campaigning. While the tale may have proved to be erroneous, its appearance on the internet still speaks volumes about Joachim's lasting impact.

By all accounts, though, Joachim is one of Christian history's most colorful characters, as well as one of its most seminal and mysterious ones. As a result, the bibliography of Joachim books is considerable, but readers interested in learning more may want to begin with such basic volumes as Delno C. West, ed., *Joachim of Fiore in Christian Thought: Essays on the Influence of the Calabrian Prophet* (New York: Burt Franklin, 1975).

6. Bernard McGinn, "Who was Joachim of Fiore?" *Frontline*, http://www.pbs.org/wgbh/pages/frontline/shows/apocalyse/explanation/joachim.html.

13

The Agency of Change

How does the Spirit work in any era? Some biblical scholars, representing a variety of theological persuasions, would say that we see the Spirit at work in events like the political upheavals, the re-ordering of governments and peoples, and the mass demonstrations and movements that one finds so many evidences of in our time.[1] Others—including some of those who try to understand the Emergence movement that is occurring in latinized Christianity today—suggest that religious and spiritual upheaval may, in fact, characterize the Spirit's most essential work. In other words, they hold that in every time and place, the Spirit—that is, God—is about movement/disruption and change/transformation.

Spirit upsets. A quarter century ago, Harvard dean Krister Stendahl provocatively wrote in the preface to his book *Energy for Life* that he hoped the Western Church, including his own Lutheran tradition, would begin experimenting with "Spirit language" for God rather than "Christ language." He also advocated for the Eastern understanding of the Trinity, contra-*filioque*, saying that to understand the procession of the Spirit from both Father and Son is to limit and narrowly define it, leaving Spirit safely within the confines of the church where only a portion of its work is accomplished.[2]

Brian McLaren—not so much the forerunner as the Martin Luther, if there ever was one, of Emergence Christianity—wrote well over a decade ago in *A New Kind of Christian* of the personal, often existentially painful, way in which people become gradually able to dislodge themselves from old paradigms of religious and spiritual life and thought as they find themselves entering new ones. McLaren reflected with these now-famous, clearly prophetic, sentences: "What if God is actually behind these disillusionments and disembeddings? What if God is trying to move us out of Egypt, so to speak, and into the wilderness, because it's time for the next chapter in our adventure? What if it's time for a new phase in the unfolding mission God intends for the people (or at least some of the people) who seek to know, love, and serve God?"[3]

Joachim of Fiore saw the Age of the Spirit—for this was the name he gave to our third and final era—as a time when leadership in ecclesial structures would be destabilized and decentered. A faithful son of the Roman Church, as well as one subservient to the pope's authority until his own death, Joachim in his writings nevertheless put much more hope in committed believers practicing active and contemplative lives of faith and practice than in institutions and pontiffs. And blessedly, according to that Calabrian monk's vision, while the first era equaled a time of fear, the second era was a time of faith, and the third era would equal a time of love.[4] Each era has its primary means of revelation. None of them is final until the very end.

One of our finest contemporary theologians, Professor Harvey Cox of Harvard Divinity School, has recently and thoroughly written of Joachim's prophecies, summarizing that what we are currently experiencing is similar to what Joachim foresaw and is surely "a profound change in the elemental nature of religiousness." In *The Future of Faith*, Cox posits three epochs thus far, clearly inspired by the taxonomy of Joachim, the last of which, according to Cox, might now be summarized as follows:

Era: The Age of the Spirit

Originating moment: The gradual crumbling of trust in the power of belief

Centrifugal force: Rapid growth of a non-hierarchical Christianity that centers around spiritual experience and hope, rather than belief

Hope and expectation: Various, uncertain, since this movement is by definition without any specific center

Circa: 1900 CE to the present[5]

Cox is an advocate for the importance of this last era, our present moment, the Age of the Spirit, and, in fact, he has been one of its champions for the better part of a half century. He summarizes: "The experience *of* the divine is displacing theories *about* it. No wonder the atmosphere in the burgeoning Christian congregations of Asia and Africa feels more like that of first-century Corinth or Ephesus than it does like that of the Rome or Paris of a thousand years later."[6]

All of this having been said, however, one must also add the obvious. Even in the Age of the Spirit, to use Joachim's term and as Cox employs it and/or in this time of Emergence Christianity, belief has not become a matter of no use and little regard. It is, and will always be, the way by which millions of religious believers like us encounter, perceive, and sort the world before our noses. Yes, it is true that reason became increasingly cold after the Enlightenment, and yes, it is also very true that Emergence and Convergence Christians today are *post-* everything related to "belief" when it is delivered in terms of propositional faith and creed. But belief discerned in the Spirit will always have its role in the living of a spiritual and religious life.

There is no question but that something enormous is going on in the religious life and in the way that we understand our place in human history. That something reflects not only old Joachim of Fiore and his prophecies, but it also anticipates a sharply different and new era, an era that already we have begun moving into. Before we carry our discussion any farther into immediate times, however, we need to look at one other component of them, one that we have hinted at but not yet truly explored.

Notes

1. See, for instance, José Comblin, *The Holy Spirit and Liberation* (Maryknoll, NY: Orbis, 1989); Lee E. Snook, *What in the World Is God Doing? Re-Imagining Spirit and Power* (Minneapolis: Fortress, 1999); Amos Yong, *Who Is the Holy Spirit? A Walk with the Apostles* (Brewster, MA: Paraclete Press, 2011); and although he is not a formally trained theologian, one also thinks of the new book by the provocative Catholic priest, Diarmuid O'Murchu, *In the Beginning Was the Spirit: Science, Religion, and Indigenous Spirituality* (Maryknoll, NY: Orbis, 2012).

2. Krister Stendahl, *Energy for Life: Reflections on the Theme "Come Holy Spirit—Renew the Whole Creation"* (Geneva: WCC Publications, 1990).

3. Brian McLaren, *A New Kind of Christian: A Tale of Two Friends on a Spiritual Journey* (San Francisco: Jossey-Bass, 2001), xi–xii.

4. Marjorie Reeves, *Joachim of Fiore and the Prophetic Future* (New York: Harper, 1977), 14.

5. Harvey Cox, *The Future of Faith* (New York: HarperOne, 2009), 1, 4–20.

6. Ibid., 20.

14

Enter the Followers
of the Prophet Muhammad

Long before the East–West split and the Great Schism, and certainly long before Joachim of Fiore's prophecies on the Age of the Spirit began filling the ecclesiastical loggia with predilections for change, the youngest of the Abrahamic faiths had begun to nip away at some of the cherished assumptions and basic structures of its siblings. What had begun as a series of revelations to an orphan-turned-merchant in Mecca had morphed, first, into a nomadic, desert-based sect throughout Arabia and then, quickly thereafter, into a world empire that was completely misunderstood by the dominant Christian world.

When Muhammad began his public ministry, there were five episcopal centers, or sees, in Christendom: Alexandria, Antioch, Constantinople, Jerusalem, and Rome. By the year 700, only one generation after Islam was firmly established, only Constantinople and Rome remained. The others had been overrun by the religious not-so-close cousins of Christianity from the east.

We still today judge the religion of the Prophet in terms of that bloody history as well as on the basis of its most extreme contemporary adherents. What Christians and Jews rarely accept about the original rise of Islam, however, is that Muhammad truly respected both faiths. He was equally possessed, though, by a sincere desire to "fix" what he saw as their errors about the nature of God. This, in fact, was why he had heard those revelations from the Divine in the first place, or so he thought.

Restorers of faith. Revealers of the true God. This is how, by their own admission, the first Muslims viewed their role in the religious world. Historically speaking, we know that they did not believe that they had founded a new religion. Rather, they thought they were reviving the religious contract that had first been inaugurated between God and Abraham. Islam was meant to be a corrective of rabbinic Judaism, which was known to Muhammad firsthand (a sizeable Jewish population existed in Medina in those days), and to Christianity, already the world's most dominant faith. The Prophet believed that both faiths had wandered away from monotheism. He believed this, in no small part, because of the *filioque* controversy.

Muhammad ibn 'Abd Allah began his prophetic activities in Mecca, where his fellow citizens almost killed him for his religious troublemaking and then, instead, forced him to move some two hundred miles away to Yathrib (today's Medina), where he lived in the Sasanian Persian Empire, beyond the reaches of the Byzantine or Later Roman Empire to the west.

In Persia, there was certainly a multiplicity of gods and pagan practices, most of them existing under the rubrics and umbrellas of Zoroastrianism, but the adherents, texts, and beliefs of Judaism and Christianity were also well known to Muhammad. Of these, he seems to have been troubled most by what he knew of the beliefs and practices of Christians. It was at about this time—roughly 610 CE—that a

Christian theologian known as Maximus the Confessor, or Maximus of Constantinople, was beginning to speak of God as "identically a monad and a triad." Surely this sort of language confused Christians themselves, let alone Muhammad.[1]

Contemporary American historian Lesley Hazleton recently summarized this period in the seventh century by saying that seemingly abstruse questions as to whether Jesus was both God and man, or God in human form—whether he had one nature or two—had become highly politicized, creating such deep rifts that the Byzantine Empire was essentially at war with itself as various provinces sided with one theopolitical entity or another.[2]

Since the Council of Constantinople in 381, Christians had felt confident in talking about God as Trinity. Or at least they felt inclined to try to articulate what that word or concept could mean. The truth of the thing, however, was that the statements of the Christian theologians of the time were all over the map. It's no wonder that other monotheists found them to be, well, contradictory.[3]

Working from outside the Christian communion (or from within it, for that matter) it would be difficult, if not impossible, to reconcile Christian claims of worshipping a monotheistic God together with statements such as those of Maximus the Confessor's or the promulgations of Chalcedon. There are, in other words, very credible and understandable reasons why Muhammad heard in his revelations, recorded as the Qur'an, that he was restoring the "religion of Abraham." How can God be unique if God is three-in-one? This new faith called Islam was polemical, aimed not only at Arabian paganism but also at what its prophet believed were the errors of straying from monotheism. Even the Arabic word for God, *al-ilah*, subsequently abbreviated as *Allah*, literally means "*the* God" and was designed "to proclaim a new unity of religion."[4] How ironic, Muhammad seems to have thought, that a religion—Christianity—that stamped out polytheism in the Roman Empire should have itself now wandered dangerously into those same waters.

Christians did not invent monotheism; they adopted and adapted it from Judaism, the world's first monotheistic religion. Christians likewise have always identified themselves as "children of Abraham." Even as the Christian Scriptures were being written down, Christians were also finding themselves inspired by Hellenistic philosophy, particularly that of Plato, who had believed in a universe with only one God. Early Christian theologian Justin Martyr put Plato's work to extensive use, remarking that it was Plato who showed him the wings of his soul, taking Justin to a place where he might contemplate the Godhead.[5] But there is this thorny matter of what Christians call the second and third persons of the Godhead. And then, of course, there was the matter of the West subjugating one of these God-persons to the other two.

Everything was up for grabs. Charges of polytheism would soon follow, and the cacophony of confusion that first called the Prophet to attempt the renewal of pure monotheism would only grow.[6] A millennium and a half later, that confusion and that cacophony are still abroad in the world. The difference now is that ours is indeed a glocalized world, and one that, because of its inherent immediacy, is increasingly intolerant of confusion. Part of the work of living into the Age of the Spirit will, for Christians, have to be the business of learning to think of that Spirit and of the Trinity itself in more theological and less biological terms. Such is not an easy assignment, but neither is it an optional one.

Notes

1. Vladimir Lossky, *In the Image and Likeness of God* (Crestwood, NY: St. Vladimir's Seminary Press, 1976), 85.

2. Lesley Hazleton, *The First Muslim: The Story of Muhammad* (New York: Riverhead, 2013), 58.

3. After 451 CE and as a result of the work of the Council of Chalcedon, Christianity—both East and West—was officially *dyophysite*. That Greek term literally means "two natures." Theologians had settled, at Chalcedon, on *dyophysite* for the Church's Christology in order to explain how Jesus Christ might be both man and God, having two natures: both human and divine, separate, distinct, but combined in one person. Thus, when Christ died on the cross it was the human nature of Christ that died, not the divine. By assuming Christ as *dyophysite*, or having two natures, the fathers at Chalcedon had also meant to stamp out forever the use of the heretical terms of *monophysite*, meaning that Christ possessed only one nature of pure divinity, and *miaphysite*, meaning that Christ was both divine and human in one single nature.

4. Diarmaid MacCulloch, *Christianity: The First Three Thousand Years* (New York: Penguin Books, 2011), 257.

5. See, for instance, the *First Apology* and *Dialogue with Trypho* of Justin Martyr. These were written between 150 and 160 CE.

6. Obviously, there are more detailed Muslim objections to the Christian Trinity than just those concerning the Spirit. Some of the more pressing ones center on the person of Christ. How, for instance, could the Divine come under human control, as Christ did during his passion? How could any part (and just the notion of *parts* is a problem) of the Divine have a beginning, as in a human birth?

15

The Simmering Pot

Like Muhammad, Joachim of Fiore was a prophet. By definition, a prophet, regardless of his or her theological affiliations, is one who receives the word of God and transmits it by means of human language to his or her fellows. But hard on the heels of Joachim's lifetime of prophecy, latinized Christianity was overtaken by another form of religious vocation: mysticism.

All religions have—and deeply revere—their own mystics, just as all of them often honor the mystics of other faiths, and for good reason. Mysticism is a mode of conversation or of knowing that exists external to the particularities of a specific theology. That is, unlike the prophet, a mystic is not a conduit. Rather, the mystic is a fiber in a substantial rug—nothing more than that—a single fiber that is part of a thread that is part of a strand that is part of the rug. And the mystic speaks, not the pattern of the rug, but the essential rug-ness of which he or she knows himself or herself to be both an integral and an unnecessary part.

The list of the men and women who were European mystics in the two and a half centuries after Joachim is a roll call of dozens, if not hundreds, of reverenced names. One thinks, for instance, of Meister Eckhart (1260–1327 CE), John Tauler (c. 1300–61 CE), and Henry Suso (1300–66 CE), who together came to be known to later generations as the Rhineland school of mysticism. There was the great Flemish mystic, John Ruysbroek (1293–1381 CE) and the enigmatic Bavarian, Henry of Nordliger, who was born in the early fourteenth century, but then suddenly disappears completely after 1352 CE, leaving a personal mystery of his own behind him. Gerard Groot (1340–84 CE) was as Dutch as his name would indicate, and no one could ever forget the most eloquent of them all, Thomas à Kempis (1380–1471 CE), with his little book and his little nook. Nor could any counting ever be complete without that most beloved of all of them, Dame Julian of Norwich (1342–1416 CE).[1]

The list goes on and on, of course, but the mystics matter to our present discussion not so much as individuals but as an aggregate. Seen in that light, they become a kind of phenomenon that spoke at a popular level to the cultural and religious mind-set that Joachim had foreshadowed and that the Reformation would ultimately have to address.

The mystics were dealing outside the bounds of doctrine. They were yearning toward and reporting on experiential, rather than epistemological or well-ordered, religion. By and large, they were also getting away with spreading their blatantly extra-ecclesial writings and speeches. By any set of definitions, they were trafficking in what was "spiritual" even if it were not "religious" in the way that Mother Church understood that term.

What the mystics had to say, moreover, was of enormous appeal to the people who gathered around them. The very fact that many of them did indeed get away with publicly proclaiming their non-doctrinal and highly spiritual talk invited other folk—not necessarily mystics, but just plain uneasy Christians—to entertain daring and previously unarticulated thoughts and possibilities about the realm of the spirit or, as the case might be, of the Spirit.

Not all the restiveness of those centuries found its outlet in disjointed and non-cohesive conversations, though. All over Europe, there were scattered groups of Christians disavowing Mother Church and organizing themselves into worshipping bodies that owed their allegiance to the movings of the Spirit, not to those of Rome. The ones best known to most of us today were groups like the Cathars, the Albigensians, the Waldensians, or even the Bogomil churches in Bulgaria, all of them more or less identical in general thrust, if not always in the small details.

By the early thirteenth century, the Cathars had managed to go so far afield and to grow so numerous and influential as to frighten Pope Innocent III into mounting a major military campaign against their communities in the south of France. Shortly thereafter, Innocent went even further and instituted the Medieval Inquisition just to make sure he had gotten all those heretical experimenters, if not by one means, then by the other.

The Cathars' doctrinal offenses were undeniably numerous, but foundational to them all was their dualism. They held that there were two Forces or gods in creation, one, God, who was good and the other, Satan, who was evil. But God was one entity—a disincarnate entity, in fact—that was pure Spirit. Catharism and its various spin-offs were clearly Gnostic and clearly heretical. Neither of those points has ever really been much in question. The point that is remarkable and pertinent, however, is that Catharism and its various presentations could not have existed, much less grown strong enough to seriously threaten the papacy and the Church, had there not been a deep-seated uneasiness among good, traditional Christians about what exactly "spirit" was and about what God was in relation to that ill-defined beingness.

The questions bubbled like a slow boil just below the surface of latinized Christianity and its teachings. In particular, there were those teachings not only about triune God, but also about the procession of one of them—of the most attractive one of them, in fact and mystically speaking—from the other two. Nor were those questions happening in an ideational vacuum. Islam and the Arabic culture that carried it had, as we have seen, begun a major push into both Africa and Europe within just a few decades of Muhammad's death. By 750 CE, the area around Cordoba in Spain had already become a major caliphate, or Islamic state, that would, in turn, spawn other or spin-off Islamic units. It was not, in fact, until 1492, that year so fated in so many ways, that indigenous royalty finally succeeded in driving the Muslims out of the western part of Europe. It would take even longer in Eastern Europe, the last Muslim armies and political units not having been successfully driven out until 1683, when much of Vienna was torched in the process.

While there were certainly differing cultural and political values involved in that centuries-long struggle with Islam, the religious or theological struggle was primarily—and as we have already noted— one about One-God-in-Three-Parts and the impenetrable question of Spirit: what It was, what It was in divine relationship, what It was in function, how It was to be known—Separately? En masse? How?[2]

Each time latinized Christianity and the cultures that it informs have gone through one of our semi-millennial upheavals, there has always been a prior period of about a century and a half that serves as a buildup of sorts to the moment when the upheaval is demonstrably present and a documentable fact. Called the "peri-" as in the peri-Transition, or the peri-Great Decline and Fall, or the peri-Great Schism, or the peri-Reformation, it is concerned with the slow disestablishment of the authority that had held both the culture and the Church steady for the previous three or four centuries.

So it was that when, by the late fourteenth century, the buildup to the Great Reformation—that is, the peri-Reformation—had begun to evidence itself, so too had the centrality of the Holy Spirit to the theology and ecclesiology that would become Protestantism.

In England, the Lollards, who were followers of John Wycliffe, were becoming more and more adamant that a clearer and more useful statement about the Holy Ghost must be formulated. In Europe, the "spiritual" Franciscans who, as an order, had always been like Joachim in believing in a new age of the Spirit, were again growing more outspoken about their beliefs. As copies of Holy Writ became more readily available, both privileged and ordinary citizens were beginning to express aloud their conviction that one of the great sins of the Church had been to usurp the Spirit's function as sole interpreter of the Scriptures.[3] Growing bodies of believers like the Anabaptists and the Munzerites were aggressively reconfiguring traditional doctrine and traditional Christian worship, claiming the Spirit and what they referred to as the "inner Light" as their authority for doing so.[4] Mysticism was beginning to crop up again. And with all of this, the desire for experiential engagement with God, the Spirit, grew into a kind of steady simmer.

There was, in all of these various and sympathetic expressions of doctrinal insurrection, a clear agreement that the Church had held Christians and Christianity hostage for centuries. By its usurpation of power over all of life, the Church had circumvented Holy Writ and produced instead politically useful interpretations of it: custom-made formulations and self-serving and self-perpetuating strictures and obscurities. But no more. No more papacy, no more magisterium, no more curia.

One of the problems—indeed, probably the central problem—with disestablishing extant and operative authority is that chaos can and does ensue, unless the emerging new thinkers, leaders, politicians, and theologians can discover—preferably, sooner rather than later—a new source of authority. Looked at logically, the authority to be established by the great Reformers should have been the Holy Spirit unmediated—or as earlier times would have said, the Holy Ghost unmediated. That did not quite happen, at least not exactly.

Luther and his fellow reformers—though the primary role in this was Luther's—in the press of their need to answer the question of "How now shall we live and in accord with which principles and rules?" turned to Scripture itself as the new base upon which authority was to rest and from which the rules of life were to flow. The leap from the rigidity of papal and curial control to unfettered control by direct engagement with the Spirit was too great to make. Maybe later, but not now.

Early on in the Great Reformation, standing in front of the Diet of Worms in May 1521, Luther delivered his immortal "Here I Stand" speech in defense of himself and of his new theology. In it, he would declare quite emphatically that he could not, and would not, follow any principle or doctrine or ecclesial officer or theological authority unless he was first convinced of the rightness of their position by what he found in Scripture and that was compatible with "plain reason."

What is more interesting, however, is what he said next: "Scripture is to be understood alone through that Spirit who wrote it, which Spirit you cannot find more surely present than in these sacred Scriptures, which he himself wrote."[5]

The Spirit had been located, at least for the time being, and *sola scriptura* would become the order of the day for the coming centuries.[6]

Notes

1. This should by no means be interpreted as suggesting that superb theologians were not also hard at work during these same centuries and on the same

questions. They were. St. Augustine, in the late fourth and early fifth centuries, had laid much of the groundwork for what these later medieval theologians would formulate.

Heavily influenced by the Cappadocian Fathers and other thinkers like Didymus the Blind and Ambrose of Milan, Augustine was a persuaded processionist whose masterful *Of the Trinity* would be a major, formative influence on men like Thomas Aquinas and those who followed him. Living and writing in the thirteenth century, Aquinas was to become a doctor of the Church and, by common consent, the greatest of the medieval theologians. It would be Aquinas who, working from both Aristotle and Augustine, would formulate an understanding of the Trinity as relationship. His line of argument would inform the subsequent centuries and extend even into our own.

2. Contemporary Christians often forget—or sometimes never even knew— that Luther himself refrained from speculating on the interrelationships of the triune persons. He demonstrated uneasiness with the word "Trinity," never including it in any of his catechisms or litanies. For more, see Christine Helmer's seminal study, *The Trinity and Martin Luther: A Study on the Relationship between Genre, Language and the Trinity in Luther's Works (1523–1546)* (Darmstadt, Germany: Verlag Philipp von Zabern, 1999).

3. One of the oddities of Aquinas's work on the Trinity is the fact that he never assumed or taught this position.

4. One of the hallmarks, especially of these two groups, was their constant cry of "The Spirit! The Spirit!" in public as well as private gatherings. And one of the almost humorous things Martin Luther was ever known to have said was spoken in the midst of such a confrontation, when he turned and scoffed, "I will not follow where their 'spirit' leads!"

Luther or no Luther, there is no question about the fact that these men and women whose "spirit" he decried were charismatics in the fullest sense of that word as we use it today. The only problem was that they were living in their sixteenth century and not in our twenty-first one. They were five hundred years too early, in other words.

5. Gerald L. Bruns, *Hermeneutics Ancient and Modern* (New Haven, CT: Yale University Press, 1992), 145; capitalization of "Spirit" has been altered.

6. The growing bibliography on the formative centrality of Trinitarian thinking, both popular and professional, to the tensions and resolutions of the Great Reformation and their aftermath is almost overwhelming. There is neither the space nor the reason to list them here, of course, but the reader who would like to pursue the matter in greater depth will find a very fine beginning place in Paul C. H. Lim's recently released *Mystery Unveiled—The Crisis of the Trinity in Early Modern England* (New York: Oxford University Press, 2012).

16

Steam Rising

As more than one wag has observed over the years, what *sola scriptura* and the locating of the Spirit's home as being within it actually did was disestablish a flesh-and-blood pope only to put a paper one in his place. It's not an entirely unfair or inaccurate summation.[1] But what Luther's position also did was to establish the primacy of the written word and, thereby, of literacy as a more or less godly virtue. And what literacy did, as a *sine qua non* of right belief and Christian discernment, was lead, straight as an arrow, to mass education, then to rationalism, and then to the Enlightenment, which latter development had been the almost inevitable result of the whole thing from the beginning. Latinized Christianity was to become a matter of the intellect, of the rational soul, of both the learned and the unlearned exegete. The culture it informed would change with it in rhythm and values, sensibilities and vogues.

As men (and women) began to read for themselves, they inevitably began to read more than Holy Writ. They read everything that came to hand. They read the scriptures of other faiths, the writings of other cultures, the startling discoveries of Newtonian physics, the political theories of free thinkers, and ultimately, of course, they read each other. Thought control was no longer entirely possible, and uniformity of shared opinion was dead. That is, *uniformity* of religious thought was dead, but not religious thought itself. Actually, in point of fact, absorption with religion and the business of thinking voraciously about it increased. Ordinary people—tradesmen and grocers, farmers and roustabouts—they all could read; they all could be irritated by authority, be it ecclesial or political; and they all cared.

Even from the earliest days of the Great Reformation itself, there had been Christians who, as convinced and practicing Christians, did more than question the Trinitarian stance that the Church had taken at Nicaea and that it had enforced and elaborated ever since. In their denial of that creedal position, some of these believers-with-questions went so far as to become openly Arian. That is, by the closing decades of the sixteenth century, many of them had become the first Unitarians, though they did not use that label at the time. Instead, because many of them were followers of a dynamic Italian theologian named Fausto Paolo Sozzini (1539–1604), they took upon themselves the sobriquet *Socinians*. As such, the majority of them inclined toward recognizing the Holy Spirit as a divine power, but not as a divinity and/or divine "person" per se. They also were the beginning of what would become a substantial and influential component of latinized Christianity, and their conceptualization of the Spirit an informing one.[2, 3]

For our purposes here, however, the most telling consequence of too much intellectualizing and formalizing of the faith was the inevitable reaction to the whole thing. In fact, the old saw that "every action has a reaction" has never been more applicable than it is as we approach the years from 1703 to 1791. Those eighty-eight years are the lifespan of John Wesley, the theologian and inspired pastor who was to grasp completely the hunger of his contemporary Christians for ecstatic and experiential worship, their need to know holiness within themselves, and their keening desire to engage the Spirit. For this broadening crowd of the spiritually starved, Wesley began in time to teach what he called "the second blessing." That is, after conversion and baptism and confirmation, and by means of discipline and prayer, a believer might, could, perhaps would receive a sudden rush of soul or spirit or Spirit that would cleanse away all sin and open its recipient to the experience of perfect love—or Love, as the case might be.

With its contagious religious fervor, Wesleyanism, which would find its own institutionalized expression in Methodism, became the progenitor in North America of the so-called Holiness Movement and then of the Revivalism of the late eighteenth and nineteenth centuries. The thrust of the Holiness Movement was unabashedly toward the acquisition of a Spirit-filled life. The believer—the skilled, ardent, prayerful, devout believer—could know and fully experience the Holy Spirit. He or she could, in fact, be "baptized" by the Holy Spirit and, thereby, receive "spiritual gifts" that would enable an even greater and richer faith path, as well as greater skills in building and expanding the Christian ministry.

But attractive and desired and yearned toward as such a transition or experience was, it remained an elusive thing that occurred in individuals and then only rarely.[4] Even Wesley had gone to his grave mourning the fact that he himself had never known or received "the second blessing." The problem was not with Wesley, however, or with those who immediately followed the path he had opened. The problem was that they were the advanced billing, but not the play itself. The play would begin in the peri-Emergence.[5]

It would begin with a Methodist minister named Charles F. Parham (1872–1929) and the forty or so enrolled students of Bethel Bible College, a small institution that Parham founded in the late fall of 1900 and housed in an old mansion in Topeka, Kansas.[6] With a reputation for disdaining denominations, Parham often declared that the only book to be studied at Bethel was the Bible, and their only teacher would be the Holy Spirit.

Together, Parham and his students all spent the month of December 1900 reading the Book of Acts. Their assigned task: To come to an understanding of the Baptism of the Holy Spirit. They read together. They studied and struggled together. And they looked inside themselves to try to search out what God was saying to them and to their generation at that particular time in history.

At the end of the month, on Monday, December 31, 1900, Parham gathered the student body of clergy and laypeople together and asked for their conclusions. Like a unanimous jury rendering a verdict, they had one: Baptism of the Holy Spirit was an indwelling of God manifested by speaking in tongues. Having discerned this message, Parham and his congregation immediately began a prayer service to offer their thoughts and words up to God. It was then, after being in prayer all night together, that on the morning of Tuesday, January 1, 1901, one of the gathered students experienced a baptism of the Holy Spirit—one that all those present knew to be genuine because she began to speak in tongues, just as had happened to the disciples of Christ in Acts, chap. 2.

It is to this small event—to this blip on the radar screen of then-Christendom—that Pentecostalism traces its roots.

The Baptism of the Holy Spirit—what a strange thing that must have sounded like to the Christian ear of a century ago! What might that mean? We still do not know exactly, nor probably will we ever know. But what we do know is that Parham met with immediate and great resistance as soon as the news leaked out that a student of his was reported to have spoken in tongues. Several weeks later, his young school was dismantled, and Parham was left wondering what to do next. Not having prayed in tongues himself, he nevertheless possessed one of the other spiritual gifts in spades: the gift of healing. He now dedicated himself to it. Traveling to Missouri, he established a healing ministry that made headlines in his day. While he was still in Missouri, Parham also inaugurated what he called the Apostolic Faith Movement, a pseudo-denomination and, ironically, the work of a man who had always disdained organized religion.

Five years later, in December 1905, Parham was in Houston, Texas, giving a series of revival talks and conducting healing services. The outpouring of positive response to his messages about the theory or theology of Baptism of the Holy Spirit was so great that he opened another fledgling Bible college, this time in Houston. Immediately enrolled at that Houston school was an African-American interim pastor by the name of William J. Seymour (1870–1922).

The son of former slaves, ("W. J.") Seymour was a large man with a powerful voice, a student of the New Testament, unmarried, and with only one eye. At that time, Parham's school was all white, just as Parham himself was white, and the laws of Texas were quite clear on the subject of mixing the races. So, Parham contrived a way around the problem. At his suggestion, Seymour would sit in the hallway to hear Parham's lessons. Afterwards, Parham was to accompany and critique Seymour as he went out into the black parts of town to practice his preaching.

And oh, could Seymour preach! Each little clapboard shack to which he brought his message rattled with energy. What seemed somewhat more theoretical for Parham was felt as absolutely possible in Seymour's telling. Only two months after finishing the short six-week course offered at the Bible college, and after receiving from Parham a minister's license in the Apostolic Faith Movement, in February 1906, Pastor Seymour was ready to venture a bit farther afield. A matron from Los Angeles who had heard Seymour preach at a small holiness church in Houston while she was visiting family asked him to come to LA and preach there. Against the advice of Parham, Seymour traveled a long way from home to southern California, intending to stay with friends for about a month.

A congregation formed quickly around Seymour and his message of baptism in the Holy Spirit. It wasn't the idea that caught people's attention, though. No, it was the activity of the Spirit directly experienced in their lives that captured them. This was a new kind of Christian life. Soon, Seymour's "congregation" was looking for a suitable building, one located in or near the heart of downtown, in what was then the African-American ghetto of inexpensive real estate. They found their suitable place at 312 Azusa Street.

The building at 312 Azusa had a long history. Originally constructed to house a small church, it had been abandoned when its originating congregation dwindled and finally ceased to be. For a while after that, it had simply stood empty and moldering, until a small business began to use it as warehousing space. After the warehousing business also closed, the old building's history grew a bit more colorful: it became a shop for selling tombstones. After the tombstone years, it had served as a stable. When Seymour and his followers found it, it was once more empty and had gone back to moldering. They decided to rent it anyway, and the rest is both ecclesial and cultural history.

Within three months of William Seymour's arrival in Los Angeles, the nearly around-the-clock services at the old stable-turned-sacred-space were attracting congregants from almost every part of the city. By their very gathering, those early converts were exercising a social insurrection and desegregation unheard of during that era of Jim Crow. Whites, blacks, Hispanics, Asians; men and women (and this more than a decade before women even received the right to vote in the United States); illiterate and educated—every social class and from more or less every known denomination sat side by side to listen to the preaching and to watch and experience speaking in tongues.

Hundreds of people were packed into that old but re-consecrated stable at all hours. Sometimes as many as fifteen hundred people would fill every rafter. The heat could be stifling, and so too could the flies left behind by the horses that had previously occupied the same space. But still they came, these hungry and strange new Christians. They came, and they experienced.

Just as Parham had known and even as they were being baptized in the Spirit, they were also receiving the gift of speaking in tongues. Moreover, they were also receiving the other Pentecostal gifts of healing and of tongues of fire among them. The Spirit had at last come again into human community to dwell there in tangible, visible, and audible form. Pentecostalism had been born, and the play had begun.

But not every Christian, much less every commentator and cleric, was persuaded that what was happening at Azusa Street was really godly, much less Christian. A reporter for the *Los Angeles Daily Times* visited Azusa Street in its first days and published this less-than-laudatory report under a headline that began, "Weird Babel of Tongues, New Sect of Fanatics Is Breaking Loose."

> Meetings are held in a tumble-down shack on Azusa Street, and the devotees of the weird doctrine practice the most fanatical rites, preach the wildest theories and work themselves into a state of mad excitement in their peculiar zeal. . . . [N]ight is made hideous in the neighborhood by the howlings of worshippers who spend hours swaying forth and back in a nerve racking attitude of prayer and supplication. They claim to have "the gift of tongues" and be able to understand the babel.[7]

While we, in the remove of over a century, may want to quip here by saying, "So much for journalistic objectivity and integrity," the significant and telling point is otherwise. The significant and telling point is that, within just a matter of days, whatever was happening in that converted stable had spread far enough and powerfully enough to attract coverage from one of the country's major newspapers—that, and the fact that it was also powerful enough to elicit such a grandeur of scorn.

Something was afoot, something that would not, and could not, be stopped.

There, in that weary old building, and unmediated by social conventions or religious strictures, a worldwide Christian movement had been sparked. And indeed "sparked" it was, for it would engage, and be engaged by, God the Spirit, and that very process would result in cataclysmic experiences the likes of which have rarely, if ever, been seen in the history of any faith.

Notes

1. What is unfair is to assume that either Luther or his colleagues ever foresaw and/or intended the doctrines of biblical inerrancy or Protestant inerrancy that evolved from the foundational cry of *sola scriptura*. It took almost three centuries and the Enlightenment to complete that transition.

2. Here again the tracing of a related theme—in this case, Unitarianism—is tangential to the main thrust of the present volume. Unitarianism is, nonetheless, the basis for a fascinating and very informative study in and of itself. This is especially true for North American Christians where Arian or Socinian positions eventuated not only in bodies like Unitarian Universalism, but also, during the years of the peri-Emergence in the nineteenth century, in the establishment of recognized communions like Jehovah's Witnesses, Christian Science, and arguably, Mormonism with its denial of the Trinity as being three co-equal persons combined in One Substance.

3. Quakerism, which traces its roots to mid-seventeenth-century England, is a direct product of these same moiling pressures, yearnings, and confusions. It, too, grew out of Arian or quasi-Arian roots. With its insistence on unprogrammed—or, put positively, on spontaneous—worship and its belief that Christ is within time and creation in order to teach His people, if only they will listen, Quakerism also is an evidencing of spiritual over creedally religious belief and praxis, though it does not engage in the classic signs of baptism by the Spirit. The influence of Quakerism on the theological thinking and early formation of Emergence Christianity was significant and, for some bodies in Emergence, remains so today.

4. There is at least one shining exception to this rather broad statement that engagement of the Spirit prior to 1900 was a matter primarily limited to individuals, and not many of them. In the 1830s during the reign of Nicholas I, there was an extended period in Russia when a communion within Russian Orthodoxy—the Molokans—underwent a major revival, the centering part of which was the manifestation to them of the Holy Spirit, along with the gifts of speaking in tongues and ecstatic dance. Not all Molokans, however, acknowledged the reality of what some of their co-religionists claimed, and the communion went into schism, the signs of the Spirit disappearing some years thereafter. It should be noted as well that the tongues of fire that were associated with the first Pentecost were not present, nor were the miraculous healings.

5. Cecil M. Robeck Jr., *Azusa Street Mission and Revival: The Birth of the Global Pentecostal Movement* (Nashville: Thomas Nelson, 2006), 4. Many of the details in these and the following paragraphs come from Robeck's work.

6. Most popular treatments of the peri-Emergence and the shaping of Emergence theology of the Spirit present—and correctly so—the work of Parham and his protégé, William Seymour, as the pivot point in which that process effectively began. Even so, we as Christians should give at least passing notice to the fact that there was a general and broad shift in sensibilities and perceptions abroad in the latinized world, of which Parham himself was initially merely a part. Many of the evidences of those shifts and/or of earlier attempts to discover and affect a new way to be of God are just simply no longer remembered. Essentially, all of them "failed," in fact, if one means by that that they did not reach beyond the sound of their spokesperson's own voice. One of those so-called false starts is still remembered and still honored, however, despite the fact that it did not make an effectual impact on the mass of its contemporaries.

There was, in the last of the nineteenth century and no more than five or six decades into the peri-Emergence, an Italian nun named Elena Guerra (now "Blessed" in accord with the saint-making processes of the Roman Catholic Church). In time, she would found the Oblate Sisters of the Holy Spirit in her native Italy. So persuaded was she of the movings of the Spirit in the world, she wrote twelve different private letters to Pope Leo. It was at her urging that, in 1897, Leo wrote an encyclical on the subject of the Holy Spirit. On the eve of the new century, he also wrote to all Catholic bishops, urging them to pray a "novena for Pentecost" to be culminated on December 31, 1900. But, as the official histories of the Catholic Charismatic Renewal Movement would soon explain, the bishops, and Catholics themselves, paid little heed to their pope in this matter. It was going to be up to their Protestant brethren to birth the Age of the Spirit.

7. "Weird Babel of Tongues, New Sect of Fanatics Is Breaking Loose," *Los Angeles Daily Times*, April 18, 1906.

The Front Story

Who can tell the Spirit's story? Who, indeed, would dare to attempt to? Of all the pieces and parts of theology and religion, faith and belief, talking and wondering, it is the nature, substance, and function of the Spirit that are sacrosanct and the most fraught with danger, should error be committed. Our forefathers and mothers have threaded their way very cautiously over the centuries, and we would do well to remember that. Yet there is a story to be told here—or better said, there is the beginning of a story, and it wants telling, albeit carefully.

Azusa Street and what happened there is of direct and very personal importance to those Christians who, by formal affiliation, are Pentecostals or Charismatics; and their number is indeed considerable. Current surveys show that there are at least as many Pentecostal Christians in the world today as there are citizens of the United States. And while available estimates may vary from a quarter billion to well over three hundred million, one thing remains very clear, namely that the numbers are growing exponentially every day. If, moreover, one adds as well those who self-identify as "Charismatics" rather than "Pentecostals," the total number of Christians whose faith tradition was either born or revived, shaped, or informed at the Azusa Street Mission increases to a half billion people—or, one full quarter of all of the Christians in the world today.[1] The influence of Azusa Street and all that has resulted from it is also of great if somewhat more diffuse importance to latinized Christianity in general and to the cultures that it informs.

No human agency could have created what happened in 1906 in Los Angeles, nor could any human agency have either contained or interrupted it. What roared out of William Seymour's re-consecrated stable was a Presence; and what that Presence brought, among other things, was freedom—the freedom to think and to know the Holy in an unfettered, unmediated way that was frightening and exhilarating and soul-sustaining all at the same time.[2] God had been among humankind from the beginning as Creator and Source and Sum. God had been among us as Divine Human and Bridge into Deity for centuries. Now, God was . . . ?

Now, God was not over there or up there or in the later and the hereafter and the someday. The story was complete—or at least had begun the move toward its completion. The kingdom of God was among us—was and is and evermore shall be. And It is pouring into Its people and out through them until all the world shall know and be subject to It and . . .

. . . and one of the things that Azusa Street also taught us was that the gift of speaking in tongues is necessary, for no human words or language can express what there was, and is, to articulate. Words, as we know them, cannot record or convey what wanted expressing. That circumstance is still valid and probably always will be, which is why all words—including ours above—still fail and wilt away. But failed and wilted as the words here may be, they nonetheless are congruent with what happened and continues to happen among Pentecostal and Charismatic Christians. They also are congruent with, and have formative implications, for both Emergence Christians and non-Emergence or traditional Christians.

To know God without a priest or pastor either funneling and directing the experience or laying down the instructions for placing the call is exhilarating. It may be frightening, in fact, for the first time or two, but ultimately it is exhilarating, not to mention habit-forming. And whether one intends it or not, inevitably it leads to circumventing much of the system. It is, in other words, not unlike what happens when one gives up telephone wires for Wi-Fi. It also leads to a certain amazement that a conversation is even happening. That, in turn, translates to a kind of reverential daring that is hungry to conduct conversation more frequently in more places and within more strange circumstances than once were even possible.

The Pentecost of 1906 was startling at first, and the subject of scathing commentary, as we know. Lifelong, convicted, and good Christians ignored it, or learned of it with indifference, or began to read magazine snippets about it, or engaged in a little parish-hall-coffee-hour fun about the crazies in the Church today, or discovered an otherwise-sensible colleague who thought something valid might actually be going on, or got hold of a book by Dennis Bennett or Jack Deere because a really responsible friend had recommended them, or . . .

. . . or finally sank into the realization that not only had something shifted, but also that the most profound change theologically and conceptually in Christianity in our era has been and is the shift toward emphasis on God, the Holy Spirit.

It would be inaccurate to say, or even imply, that Azusa Street bears the whole credit for that shift, just as it would be inaccurate to act as if the implications of that and consequent shifts were limited to Christianity. Neither of those things is true. Azusa was only one part of the peri-Emergence, though admittedly one of its more discrete and certainly more dramatic ones. What Azusa did do, however, was to help in a substantial way to open the floodgates for Christians, and by extension to Christianized culture in general, to non-hierarchal experimentation, to an openness to perceived as opposed to structured reality, and to conversational candor that enjoyed an ever-lessening fear of social and political reprisal.

This new and burgeoning freedom to speak of the Spirit and to wonder at a dramatic new way of knowing extended over the decades of the twentieth century into questions about doctrinalized religion in general, about institutional Church, and about pragmatic rather than inspired authority. It extended, in other words, to a whole list of questions that, at their core, looked remarkably like those that had plagued Luther five hundred years earlier, when he had not known exactly how to engage and/or where to place the Holy Ghost. There were, however, two or three other significant new twists to the road.

During the second half of the last century, post-Holocaust Judaism was received into mainstream Christian culture, especially in the United States, with more cordiality than it had ever enjoyed previously. The result was a ready exchange by default, if not intention, between the two faiths, an exchange that at times could become almost a blending. At the same time, as post-war concern for equality of rights and full citizenship grew all over North America, so too did an awareness of indigenous peoples and, most particularly and popularly, of native spirituality with its mystical engagement of the "Spirit"—an engagement and a Spirit free of doctrine and of particularities.

In the United States especially, changes in immigration laws opened North America's doors to new citizens of Asian descent, and in their coming, many of them brought with them Buddhism and Vedantic philosophies, with rich traditions of spiritual and, in some of their divisions, non-theistic, aphysical experience. At the same time, while relations with Islamic culture as a political construct grew more strained in most parts of the Christian world, so too did the need to know Islam as a faith. The inevitable result of increasing knowledge and familiarity was the discovery not only of similarities of principles but, and perhaps most foundational, of a congenial mysticism or spirituality in the writings of men like Rumi and Hafiz, or the Sunni scholars.

Over those same and earlier decades, psychology had grown—exponentially, in fact—from a pseudo-science of gentlemanly fascination to a formal discipline that spun off into and/or matured with other new disciplines like psychiatry and neuro-chemistry, neuro-biology and neuro-pharmacology, etc., all of which opened the world of the mind and the psyche and then asked, by default, where now and what are the soul and its longings in all of this? And then mind and psyche received unnaturally gifted communicators designed for a television age in the forms of Joseph Campbell and Bill Moyers.

In sum, both in North America and the other parts of latinized Christian culture, we passed in the twentieth century through decades of upheaval about what faith was and how it should or should not be structured, about what subjective experience is and how it should be employed, about who/what/how it is that "knows" the aphysical, about God as ground of being for all creatures, and, in the sum of it all, about what the non-historical, inconceivable Spirit of God is that moves across the waters from which we physically come and to which we all return.

The decades of unease and the loss of absolute knowing would make atheists of some of us and agnostics out of others of us. Of many of us, those decades would make the more-difficult-to-define "nones," and of many more of us, the much more outspoken spiritual-but-not-religious. But those decades would also make a new kind of Christian out of essentially all of us.[3]

Either we would become refurbished and more appreciative of what had been before the chaos began, in which case, we would give ourselves over to refining and reverencing the institution and institutions that had conveyed our heritage to us and mediated our theological understandings for us.

Or we would remain where we were within that beloved structure and polish and support it with gratitude and renewed affection, as well as with our substance and influence.

Or we would remain Pentecostals or Charismatics by inherited custom, or become one by conversion in the face of changing theology and pneumatology.

Or we would become, like many of our fellow citizens, spiritual within a Christian context, but not religious in a formalized or affiliated one.

Or we would move along the tracks and open lines of recently discovered human commonality to a Christian universalism that seeks to find in all religions an equal way to God.

Or we would become some variant of any of those broad categories.

Or we could become a new kind of Christian, one that has not been before, one that is the first fruits, so to speak, of Joachim's Age of the Spirit and that is a kind of convergence of believers drawn from all the others into another and unknown vortex.[4] We could become Emergence Christians.[5]

Whatever we are and by whatever communion label we categorize and govern ourselves, all of us who call ourselves Christian today and for many days to come are going to have to wrestle, whether we wish to or not, with the foundational questions of What/Who is the Holy Spirit? What, indeed, is the Trinity Itself? And if, like our ancestors, we cannot answer those two questions—and we may not be able to—how are we to understand this new, or perhaps better said, renewed Presence? How now shall we worship? How now shall we live into this new era, this Age of the Spirit, in which we find ourselves?

No one knows, of course, but that ignorance does not grant us any relief from the fearful solemnity of the questions, nor does it grant us any release from the necessity of dealing with them. And because Emergence Christianity in all its varying presentations is a product of these times and, as a result, is the most unencumbered movement among us, it is also the nimblest of us as well. So it is that at least some of the answers and much of new Christian theology will come from Emergence and Emergence thought. Certainly there are evidences of that already.

While Emergence is clearly the most nimble and unencumbered movement within latinized Christianity, it also enjoys one other—and very telling—advantage over the other communions in that grouping. That is, it not only enjoys the shared heritage and tradition of the first millennium of the faith, but it has unprejudiced access to the treasures and traditions of Orthodoxy that were lost to much of Latin Christianity a thousand years ago in the Great Schism. Ironically, or perhaps providentially, the greatest treasure—the signatory characteristic—of Orthodoxy has been its non-manipulative reverence for the mysteries of the Spirit. If the Spirit is to be known and engaged and wholly honored among us, then it is to Orthodoxy first that Emergence theology has turned.

Orthodox theology has always assumed a progression of Christian experience, both individually and corporately, from the kataphatic to the apophatic. Kataphatic theology has characterized latinized Christianity in all the centuries since the Great Schism. Some would even argue that a Latin proclivity for the kataphatic was part of what led to the Schism in the first place. Be that as it may, kataphatic theology seeks always to define and describe what God is. Apophatic theology, by contrast, seeks to know God in terms of what God is not. That is, as either the individual believer or the corporate body moves deeper into union in prayer with the Beingness of God, they are drawn more deeply into communion with the ineffable and transported ever more deeply into the mystery whose beauty would be defiled by overmuch defining and describing.

Emergence Christianity finds in this distinction much that is cordial to its own theology and especially to its way of approaching the Spirit and, most certainly, to its way of talking and theorizing about the Trinity. The Trinity, which is prior in any real discussion of the Spirit, is probably best conceptualized in Emergence thought as like unto fire. That is, fire has no disunity or separateness. It is. It is fire and, as such, is multi-hued flame of reds and yellows and blues. Its property is heat. In none of these is there division, and in all of this non-division there is variousness that can be seen and touched and consumed by, but never grasped nor rendered constant.[6]

One of the felicitous parts of this way of being with the Trinity is that it avoids, almost unconsciously, the trap of thinking biologically about the Trinity and its components. The "persons" stance of traditional Christianity withers away, exposing itself as a kind of rhetorical trap or *cul de sac* and opening the way to thinking theologically instead. It would be false to say that that shift has entirely happened. It is very accurate, however, to say that the process leading to it has begun.[7]

It is also quite accurate to say that among many and probably most Emergence leaders even the need to think theologically about either the Trinity or the Spirit is often lost. It has been drowned out in the exponentially expanding reality of the Spirit's presence among us, drowned out in the same way that erotic love drowns out any need for discussion of physical particulars.

Some Emergence leaders and theologians are moving away from biological thinking so completely as to resist even such talk as this. They have moved instead to asking us to know God as an activity rather than as an entity. They celebrate the "I am" of God's first declaration of His identity to Moses as being a declaration of "Is-ness" that is everywhere and always present.

There is, in all of this, clearly no uniformity of thought, even as there is some obvious urgency in the inquiry. As this new form of Christianity and this new way of being Church and Kingdom mature, they, like their predecessors in earlier upheavals, must soon come to address the question of authority—to address the question of how now shall we live and by whose definitions of right and wrong, correct and incorrect, holy and heretical.

When they and/or we fully engage that dreaded question, it will be in terms of the Spirit and of holy discernment. The center of our new authority will not lie, as it did in earlier presentations, with the Church fathers and mothers or with Church councils, not with politico-ecclesial hierarchies, nor even in *sola scriptura* and inerrancy as it is popularly defined. Rather, it will lie within the realm of the Spirit and an awe-filled, discerning intercourse with It.

Writing some eighteen centuries ago, Basil the Great expressed what would have been the crux of that problem for his own time. "What," he asked, "are the energies of the Spirit? Their extent cannot be told, and they are numberless. How can we comprehend what is beyond the ages?"[8]

His question was a sound one, and its truth appertained from his own time in the fourth century right up until shortly before our own. The difference between our world and Basil's, though, is that the Spirit now wants to be known as It was known in the days of our beginning. And in that truth lies the Front Story for us as this Age's people of God.

Notes

1. "Pentecostal Resource Page," Pew Forum on Religion and Public Life, modified October 5, 2006, accessed July 22, 2011, http://www.pewforum.org/Christian/Evangelical-Protestant-Churches/Pentecostal-Resource-Page.aspx.

It is also worth noting here that some several years ago, Pew began to employ the term "Renewalists" for naming the larger whole that occurs when demographers put Pentecostals and Charismatics into a shared grouping. The result has not only been a considerable reduction in rhetorical awkwardness but also a formal and very useful recognition of the shared sensibilities that bind the two groups to one another.

2. Tanya Luhrmann, a psychological anthropologist and professor of anthropology at Stanford University, is a brilliant student of these shifts and changes, as well as a gifted recorder of their presentations in real life among real people. In particular, interested readers may want to see her volume, *When God Talks Back* (New York: Knopf, 2012), in this regard.

3. While we speak, in all of this, about Christians, because that is the focus of the present discussion, it is important that we recognize as well that these same cultural forces and swirling questions have impacted other faith groups as well, especially Judaism.

4. The term, "a new kind of Christian," has become almost a byword or specific descriptor for Emergence Christians. It takes its importance and origin from a pivotal book by Brian McLaren, *A New Kind of Christian: A Tale of Two Friends on a Spiritual Journey* (San Francisco: Jossey-Bass, 2001) and was reenforced by the publication in 2008 of Tony Jones's *The New Christians: Dispatches from the Emergent Frontier* (San Francisco: Jossey-Bass).

5. The choice of the word *convergence* here is not accidental. Within Emergence Christianity or running alongside of it—and no one is quite sure yet which is the accurate assessment—is a move on the part of some Christians toward a universalism that is non-doctrinal, empathetic, and immediate. Those moving in this direction now refer to themselves as Convergents and to their movement as Convergence Christianity. Their numbers are drawn primarily from Progressive Evangelicals, Progressive Roman Catholics, Missional mainliners, and social justice–oriented Pentecostals and Evangelicals. The curious readers may find a very complete statement of Convergence postures at Brian Berghoef, "A New Convergence," *The Musings of a Pub Theologian* (blog), December 12, 2012, http://pubtheologian.com/2012/12/12/a-new-convergence/.

6. There is much seminal work being done in this area, but perhaps the most complete and most accessible introduction and overview is Ian Mobsby, *The Becoming of G-d: What the Trinitarian Nature of God Has to Do with Church and a Deep Spirituality for the 21st Century* (London: YTC Press, 2008).

7. One variation on this conceptualizing is at least semi-biological or "personed." *Perichoresis* is a Greek word that originally had to do with the relationship of performing parts among themselves and with the whole they were and were

creating. It was especially understood to describe dancers and the dance and is, quite obviously, the root word for our English *choreography*.

As a theological conceptualization, *perichoresis* has a sometimes tenuous history of usage in Christian thought. It was first applied to Christian theology, apparently, by Gregory of Nazianzus. John of Damascus, in the early eighth century, employed it more fully and, more or less, popularized it as naming a "cleaving together" within the Trinity.

A kind of either "person-ness" or "entity-ness" is implied by the very logic of such a definition, of course, but the term fell into relative disuse until recently, where it has reappeared in the teaching of some of our most gifted and influential theologians and thinkers like Miroslav Volf and Jürgen Moltmann.

8. See Augustine, *Serm.* 81.8.

Appendix A

Other Major Heresies

In the earliest days of the Church, when Christians were only a generation or two removed from Christ among them on earth, almost all theological discussion tended to address not the matter of the Holy Spirit but instead the more immediate concern of God, the Son. Looked at logically, this choice of emphasis was as reasonable as it should have been predictable.

The concept of God as ultimate source and male progenitor was firmly in place by the Great Transformation. There had already been at least two thousand years of ongoing conversation with Him and about Him. That is not to say that the Spirit had not also been present and acknowledged for millennia as well. Certainly, the Spirit quite definitely had been, and there was also the tradition of Spirit-speaking prophets to give some definition and much reassurance. But the Son was the promised fulfillment at last of what it all had been about to start with. Who was—in fact, who is—this God-Man, this Jesus? they asked. What was it that happened among us not so long ago? How are we to understand it? How should we approach it/It?

In the first five centuries of the Church's formation, there were basically four major, non-Gnostic streams of thought about God the Son and, by extension, the Trinitarian nature of God, and each of them would indeed come in time to be rejected as heretical. Beyond even that fact is the sad truth that each of these major aberrations also spawned numerous proponents and numerous variations of its core concepts, each of which was likewise rejected.

Adoptionism, in particular, had many proponents, yet it is not at all clear who first formulated the ideas or concepts behind it. Possibly those ideas just simply emerged, for of all the heretical doctrines of the Son and, by extension, of the Trinity, Adoptionism, along with its half-brother *Monarchianism*, is undoubtedly the simplest to comprehend and to defend. Both taught that the only God Who properly exists is what the beloved community called God, the Father. Jesus, consequently, was a man, albeit one who had been adopted by God. In such a construct, the Holy Spirit becomes just another name for God's special grace and presence.

Paul of Samosata, who was elected as bishop of Antioch about 260, was to become probably the most colorful and most vocal proponent of Adoptionism and Monarchianism. As a result, in 269, some seventy of his fellow bishops assembled at Antioch and deposed him for his efforts. Truth be told, history would suggest that Paul's flamboyance and personal wealth may have played as large a part in his ousting as his theology did. We will never know the truth of that, of course, but we can and do know that, half a century later, in 325 CE, the First Council of Nicaea roundly rejected both Adoptionism and Monarchianism, labeling them as heretical.

The third of the Great Heresies, *Nestorianism*, gets its name from Nestorius, who was patriarch of Constantinople from 428 to 431 CE.

Nestorius's basic, if fallacious, argument was that Christ had two loosely connected natures or substances. That is, Nestorianism, which flourished until the sixteenth century in Eastern Christianity and traces of which can still be found today, holds that Jesus was fully human and was simply "occupied" by divinity for the years of the Christ's physical life. Jesus was, in a sense, taken over by God until such time as He was no longer needed.

Probably the thing about all of this that most angered many fifth-century Christians was the fact that Nestorius argued that the Virgin could not, by this line of theological argument, be called the *theotokos*, the mother of God, since she was no more than the mother of a physical baby who would later be the dwelling place of the Divine for a brief period. So odious was this understanding of the Trinitarian quandary that by 431 it was roundly condemned by the First Council of Ephesus (and once again some twenty years later at the Council of Chaledon, lest there should have been any question about the matter), and Nestorius himself was deposed, declared a heretic, and ultimately sent into exile in Egypt.

There is considerable debate to this very day about the nature of the Virgin's place in Christian theology. The argument has often been made that for millions of devout, non-Protestant Christians, the Virgin, in practice and at a lay level, is a kind of fourth part of the tripartite Trinity. This peculiar lack of definition about Mary's role, while it depended originally from a lack of definition about the nature of God the Son, has taken on a kind of new urgency in our times as Christianity tries to counter Islam's accusations against what the latter sees as the former's latent polytheism. We have, of necessity, returned to this difficulty from time to time in these pages, as we must, inevitably, in our lives.

Of the four major non-Gnostic heresies and their variations of heresy about the Trinity that assailed the Church during its formative first half millennium, none was more divisive, however, than *Monophysitism*. Ultimately, it would split the Western and Eastern Churches away from communion with the Oriental churches, some branches of which persisted for centuries in upholding it as orthodox doctrine. Monophysitists—*monos* is Greek for *one*, and *physis* means *nature*—held that Christ had only one nature, and this single nature, Monophysitists taught, was either wholly divine or else some sort of synthesis of divine-human that nevertheless would have made true human weakness impossible. And this, many in Western and Mediterranean Christianity found to be an intolerable expression of the nature of the Trinity.

Appendix B

The Ecumenical Councils

While looking in any detail at the seven ecumenical councils falls outside of the main concerns of this book, a list of them in aggregate, along with some brief commentary, may be helpful.

First we must acknowledge that there is not universal agreement nowadays amongst the major divisions or communions of Christendom about which councils are still to be accepted. There is, however, no question that they did occur, nor is there any question about the fact that governance by council rather than by ordained hierarchy was the original *modus operandi* of the Church. One of the more poignant ironies of Church history is, by the way, that Nicaea both opens and closes the era of conciliar Christianity.

The seven ecumenical councils are:

(First) Council of Nicaea, 325 CE
(First) Council of Constantinople, 381
Council of Ephesus, 431

Council of Chalcedon, 451

Second Council of Constantinople, 553

Third Council of Constantinople, 680

Second Council of Nicaea, 787

The Third Ecumenical Council, which was convened in Ephesus in 431, centered almost entirely around the Nestorian controversy that was besieging the Church at that time. Nestorius, who held the influential post of patriarch of Constantinople, was deeply opposed to the assignation of the Greek word, *theotokos*, "God-bearer," to Mary, the mother of Jesus. He argued instead that Jesus was two more or less connected persons or personages in one body. That is, he taught that divinity entered humanity without default to either the incarnated Deity or the hosting humanity.

If that were true, then Mary simply bore a child like any other child, except for the fact that this particular child was later taken over and occupied by God. And if that were true, then she could hardly be called the Mother of God, for God was not involved until later in the life of the human male named Jesus.

Nestorius, of course, lost this one personally, being deposed from the patriarchy and ultimately exiled. His ideas, which were declared heretical by the Third Ecumenical Council, continued to live on, albeit very discretely, and eventually came to be accepted as doctrinal in some non-Mediterranean Christian communities. Beyond that, Nestorius's concepts, or variations of them, are still private and unexamined parts of the Christology of many Western Christians who, never having heard of Nestorius, are nonetheless troubled by the same questions and inconsistencies that troubled him. Not the least of these are, of course, the questions of who Mary was, what her essence was, and what her role in Christian faith and praxis now is.

The Fourth Ecumenical Council was convened twenty years later in 451 in Chalcedon, part of today's Istanbul, in the eastern portion of ancient Christendom. In many ways, Chalcedon is the most sorrowful of the Church's seven ecumenical councils. Certainly it is the one at which Christianity lost its youthful naïveté and began to evidence its passage into a stormy adolescence, for it was at Chalcedon that doctrinal differences first began overtly to separate the Church into Western Christianity and Eastern Christianity.

Put another and equally valid way, it was at Chalcedon that the growing secular and political tensions between the western and the eastern portions of the empire first found religious expression in doctrinal fights. No religion, either then or now, can stand separate from and impervious to the secular context in which it is. Likewise, one of the major hallmarks of a maturing religion is its shift from being simply a factor to being considered in the larger secular conversation to becoming an instrument, barometer, and map for everything, secular or religious.

Religiously, politically, socially, and culturally, what lay ahead for the Mediterranean world at Chalcedon—what was already hovering in the offing—was the Great Decline and Fall of the sixth century. Scholars, working all these many centuries later, still mark Ephesus and Chalcedon as ominous salvos in the lead-up to the Great Decline and Fall—as clear harbingers of the disaster that, after a century and a half of massive upheavals, would ultimately destroy most of the givens of life as it had been for centuries and then reconfigure all of them.

The Fifth Ecumenical Council of the Church was also the Second Council of Constantinople, or vice versa, according to one's point of view. In any event, it was convened in the spring of 553 and was, far and away, the shortest council ever held as well as, arguably, one of the shortest "official" gatherings in all of Christian history. It lasted less than a month and, in essence, was really more a matter of housecleaning than innovative construction. That is, it was principally about the business of tidying up Nestorianism yet once again. As a council, it re-iterated the positions taken at Ephesus in 431, but with added insistence on the necessity for their absolute adoption.[1]

The Third Council of Constantinople, held in 680–81, became known also, in later church history, as the Sixth Ecumenical Council. In substance or focus, the council was held to debate, and ultimately condemn, the notion that Jesus had possessed both human and divine wills. As a rare heresy, that one was known as *monothelitism* but, even as a heresy, it was not without appeal. The idea of two wills or levels of operative intention within the Son was a way, on the part of some churchmen, to avoid the two-substances and/or condemned Nestorian theology while still in some way explaining the contradictions or confusions of God/Man in one human flesh and one Holy Trinity.

The significance of Third Constantinople lies as much, however, in its circumstances as in its content. This Sixth Ecumenical Council was the first to be held in a world increasingly informed by Islam. Jerusalem had fallen into Muslim hands in 637, and the Christian patriarch, Sophronius, had surrendered the city and his domain to the Rashidun caliph in that year. Thereafter, clarity about Christian doctrines and practice had taken on a new urgency, both culturally and theologically. The charge of Christian polytheism was now finding its expression in very real political and cultural realignments in the world as the bishops and Church fathers understood it.

The Second Council of Nicaea—or Seventh Ecumenical Council of the Church—was convened in 787. What it did is perhaps less spectacular than were the reasons behind its doing so. What Second Nicaea did was declare that, contrary to earlier rulings by the bishops and councils, it was right, proper, and a good and worthy thing to venerate icons. What it did in substance, in other words, was declare iconoclasm to be heretical. What it did in implication, however, and perhaps more important, was to reach out for unity across the great East/West divide that was growing with frightening rapidity in both the Church and the world at large.

Less than a century earlier, in 689, the insertion of the *filioque* into occasional Western recitation of the Nicene Creed had given formal and tangible evidence of the abyss's widening presence, and if the symbolic chasm of double procession would never be undone, it could maybe at least be bridged. Some token could perhaps be offered, some peace offering of estranged, but still operative, brotherhood. The East desperately wanted its icons, and that became a vulnerability the Western bishops were willing to accommodate for the sake of a more united front in troubled times. Indeed, *sic simper est.*

The Second Council of Nicaea was not only the seventh of the Church's ecumenical councils, but it was also the last gathering of the Church Universal. Those seven councils, stretching from Nicaea in 325 to Second Nicaea in 787, were to become, ever afterward, the sum total of essential religious authority for Orthodox churches throughout the world. After Second Nicaea, and despite their united condemnation of iconoclasm there, the two bodies—East and West—would enter into the first stages of what until the closing years of the twentieth century had appeared to be irreparable rupture.

The Great Schism that would formally and viciously separate East from West and Orthodox Church from Latin Church were almost two hundred and thirty years in the offing still when Second Nicaea met. After Second Nicaea, however, the two communions never met again in shared council, nor would either side of their divide ever thereafter acknowledge the orthodoxy or rightness of the doctrinal and ecclesial positions that the other would evolve over the coming centuries. Each would convene its own councils for the discussion and ultimate determination of the correct expression of the faith, but never again would actions on such issues be taken by all the parts of the Church in concert with each other.[2] The East would take its icons, and the West would soon come to once again forbid them. The *mysterium* and the mystical would find their principal home in the East, while the declarative, didactic, and rendered would settle down and domesticate in the West.

For their own part, when the churches of Western Christendom chose to move beyond the patterns of the Jerusalem Conference and the seven ecumenical councils, they began as well the process of altering the authority and leadership model of the Church itself. Subtly, but irrevocably, the West with its papacy and its increasing centralization in Rome moved toward the assumption that authority in matters theological and ecclesial must emanate from the top down, rather than from the bottom up or, put another way, vertically rather than horizontally. Just over a millennium or so later and in our own time, Emergence Christians would join Eastern and Orthodox Christians in questioning the validity not only of that shift but also of the concept or principle behind it.

Notes

1. We should note here that it was at Ephesus that the "hypostatic union" was officially affirmed as the orthodox way of explaining how Christ's two natures, human and divine, were both essential (of the same *hypostasis*) to his person-hood from eternity.

2. The whole business of ecumenical councils is as convoluted as any part of established religion could ever hope to be. According to Orthodoxy, it is the churches—and only those churches—who acknowledge the seven ecumenical councils and who are in communion with the patriarchates of Constantinople, Alexandria, Antioch, and Jerusalem that are the purest form of the Christian Church. It is they, and they alone, who retain the true Christianity that emerged out of Judaism and the way of Jesus two thousand years ago.

Not only does Western Christianity not agree with that position, but it also refers to the seven councils as being only the *first* seven of the Church's many councils, all of the subsequent ones having been convened by the West and not including any Eastern theologians or churchmen. To further complicate matters, many Protestant bodies do not admit of the legitimacy of all of the seven that were convened. Lutheranism and Presbyterianism, for example, accept only the first four councils as efficacious, and only Anglicanism, among the divisions of the Church born out of the Great Reformation, honors all seven.

So hidden now is this fundamental rift in the Church Universal that today's most prominent Orthodox thinker and priest—Metropolitan Kallistos Ware—disturbed a number of even professional religionists when he insisted, in an interview with the editor of *Christianity Today*, on referring only to "the seven ecumenical councils" (David Neff, "The Fullness and the Center: Bishop Kallistos Ware on Evangelism, Evangelicals, and the Orthodox Church," *Christianity Today*, July 2011, 38).

Appendix C

Some Informing Differences between Western and Eastern Christian Practice

It is often said that Christianity, Eastern and Western, has differed more over the proper dating of Easter than any other ecclesial issue. This may be true. However, the praxis problems, which began as early as the 160s CE, were as much about a long list of ritual observances, practices, and dates as they were about when Easter falls. In the East, Easter was to continue its link to the Jewish Passover, meaning that it should always come after the spring equinox, on the first Sunday after the full moon. Thus, the Jewishness and humanity of Jesus were emphasized. In the West, a more complicated lunisolar calendar was used, which downplayed the connection of Easter to Pascha.

The lengths and proper days for fasting and whether or not Christ or His apostles ever actually commanded the keeping of feasts and festivals were just two of the other issues on the table almost from the beginning. And then the question behind the questions always was and has been: How important is it for the worldwide Church to agree on these matters, to show a consistent "face" to the world? The tendency always has been for the leaders in the West to say, *absolutely*, while those in the East are less likely to assume that uniformity of opinion and practice reflected on the import of the faith itself.

And there is the fact that Greek and Byzantine Christians use their everyday leavened bread for the communion meal. The Greek New Testament, after all, speaks of Jesus taking regular bread (*artos*), not the far more unusual thing of unleavened bread, and breaking it. The West models its praxis, however, after the Jewish practice of no leavening for this feast of feasts, not to mention that Western Christians also choose to call the meal the *Mass*.

And from the beginning almost, there has been the matter of whether to shave or not to shave. Social differences play an enormous, unacknowledged, and sometimes almost embarrassingly ludicrous role in the great arguments of history. The wearing of beards, for example, became a serious bone of contention between East and West and played a symbolic role in helping to separate the two. Generally speaking, Greeks wore and adored them (think: Socrates), while Latins believed that clean-shaven chins showed strength, virility (think: Julius Caesar). By the sixth and seventh centuries, clergy in the East were expected to wear beards. They showed wisdom and culture. In contrast, in the eleventh century, Pope Gregory VII actually threatened any clergy who refused to shave with sanctions. A century later, Joachim of Fiore would even argue that the entire issue was prefigured by the facial coiffure of the biblical patriarchs Esau and Jacob.[1]

Then there is the problem of competing saint calendars in East and West. As the Normans or Latin West began to control more and more Byzantine territory throughout Europe, they often repressed

Greek saints in favor of Latin ones, just as they often imposed the use of unleavened bread for Holy Communion.

These differences, along with many others, were understandably perceived as a serious liturgical—but also moral and spiritual—affront by Greek Christians. The wounds of filial betrayal at one time were so deeply felt that, in the years leading up to the Great Schism, when the patriarch in Constantinople first learned of them, he once retaliated by forcing some of the Latin churches within his reach to be shuttered.[2]

Other less fundamental areas of separation also continue to exist between East and West, but the central point to be made here is that culture and theology can never be entirely severed, one from the other. Instead, each informs the other, and that is as true today as it was in the days of the Great Schism.

Notes

1. Henry Chadwick, *East and West: The Making of a Rift in the Church* (New York: Oxford University Press, 2005), 12.

2. Andrew Louth, *Greek East and Latin West: The Church AD 681–1071* (Crestwood, NY: St. Vladimir's Seminary Press, 2007), 307.

Appendix D

A Few Words from the Greek

We have spent a fair amount of time throughout the preceding pages describing how one simple Latin phrase (*filioque*) impacted the Church West and East. Here, it is at least worth pausing briefly over eleven pivotal theological words from ancient Greek that each played a part in the posturing as well.

Aitia means "reason" or "cause," as in an efficient, material, formal cause. This is the word that was most often used by Eastern theologians throughout the Middle Ages to describe the Father as *aitia* of both Son and Holy Spirit. To see this word functioning in Scripture, apart from any notion of Trinity, see Luke 8:47 and Acts 10:21.

Dia means "through" or "by means of," as in the English words *diagonal* and *diagnosis*. Here are two examples of how *dia* was translated in the King James Bible: "Now all this was done, that it might be fulfilled which was spoken of the Lord by [*dia*] the prophet" (Matt. 1:22); and "This fellow said, I am able to destroy the temple of God, and to build it in [*dia*] three days" (Matt. 26:61). More relevant for our purposes, *dia* is a distinguishing word in the *filioque* controversy according to Western figures who used it to explain the mediating role the Son plays in the procession of the Spirit from the Father.

Dyophysite is a post-biblical Greek term that literally means "two natures" and names a theological position, as well as one who believes this position. At the Council of Chalcedon in 451, the church settled on *dyophysite* in its official Christology in order to explain how Jesus Christ might be both man and God, having two natures: both human and divine, separate, distinct, but combined in one person. Thus, when Christ died on the cross it was the human nature of Christ that died, not the divine. This in contrast to *monophysite*, that Christ possessed one divine nature, and *miaphysite*, that Christ was both divine and human in one single nature.

Ek is a preposition used to connote a movement from inside to outside. It usually literally means "out from among" (as distinguished from "away from," which would be the preposition *apo*). This preposition was often used by Western theologians to argue the *filioque* cause even more vigorously than with *dia*.

Homoousios is a theological term that does not appear in the Bible and literally means "same substance." The term was condemned by the Synods of Antioch in the third and fourth centuries as a reference for God because of its origins in pagan philosophy. But the Emperor Constantine championed it at the First Council of Nicaea in 325 CE, and the Nicene Creed uses the word, contra-Arius, to describe the Son as "same in being or substance" to the Father. Theologians in the East were uneasy with this, since *homoousios* had been previously used by the Syrian bishop of Antioch, Paul of Samosata, as part of the Monarchian heresy.

Homoiousios is another theological term that doesn't appear in Scripture, but means "similar in substance." It was favored by some in the East who rejected *homoousios*, for instance, by the supporters of Arianism after the Council of Nicaea.

Hypostasis is most often translated "person" today, but more literally means "underpinning," "foundation," or "sediment." This term became common at ecumenical councils after First Nicaea when it was championed by the Cappadocian Fathers, who used it to express the belief that in the Godhead there are three *hypostases* (the plural form of the noun) in one *ousia* (see below for this noun). The Eastern Church has always preferred this word to describe the Trinity, *hypostasis*, often understanding it to be like "energies" or "actualities" more than "persons." The italicized phrases in this passage from Hebrews have been said to express this idea:

> Long ago God spoke to our ancestors in many and various ways by the prophets, but in these last days he has spoken to us by a Son, whom he appointed heir of all things, through whom he also created the worlds. He is *the reflection of* God's glory and *the exact imprint of* God's very being, and he sustains all things by his powerful word. When he had made purification for sins, he sat down at the right hand of the Majesty on high. (Heb. 1:1–3)

When, in chap. 3 ("The Great Enigma"), we discussed the personae of the Trinity, comparing them to characters in a play, we would have used the word *hypostasis* had we been writing for theologians. As one Eastern theologian succinctly puts it, "it is only according to Its [the Trinity's] hypostatic powers that the Divinity is knowable and determined."[1] This, in contrast to the Trinity's essence, which remains unknowable. It is also from this word that the theological phrase/idea of "hypostatic union" comes from, used to describe the equal mixing of human and divine in the person of Jesus Christ.

Ousia means "substance" or "essence," although the twentieth-century philosopher Martin Heidegger believed that the true understanding of the word was "being." *Ousia* is the word used for the Godhead by the early Church fathers and mothers. It does not appear in the New Testament except for in the parable of the Prodigal Son, when the wayward son asks his father to divide out and give to him his portion of goods (*ousia*). In this sense, as St. Basil says, *ousia* "is the general" and *hypostasis* is the particular.[2] It was Origen (d. 251) who first readily used the term to describe the Trinity, writing that God is one *genus* of *ousia*. A more philosophical meaning of the noun comes from St. John Damascene when he defines *ousia* as "all that subsists by itself and which has not its being in another"—in other words, God alone.[3]

Parakletos means "comforter," "advocate," and "helper." It is a Koine Greek term with no equivalent in the Hebrew Scriptures and was understood by Christians to mean the third person of the Trinity, and the activity of the same, simultaneously, since the late first century CE. See Acts 1:5, 8, etc., and John 14:16, 26, etc.

Perichoresis, meaning "around" and "containing," is another post-biblical term that originated in the writings of Gregory of Nazianius. It is a theological term that attempts to describe the mutual inter-penetration and intimacy characterizing the Godhead within itself. Twentieth-century theologians Jürgen Moltmann and Miroslav Volf have renewed its use in our day.

Pneuma means "wind," "breath," or "spirit." Most uses of this noun in the New Testament show the word translated using one of the lower-case, as in: "Her spirit returned, and she got up at once" (Luke 8:55a). But this is also the Greek word occasionally translated in the New Testament with a capitalized *S* for the third person of the Trinity: "For if you live according to the flesh, you will die; but if by the Spirit you put to death the deeds of the body, you will live" (Rom. 8:13). Importantly, it is a noun with no gender, which is why, while God the Father and God the Son are properly masculine, God the Spirit is most properly rendered neuter: He, He, and It.

Notes

1. Philip Sherrard, *The Greek East and the Latin West: A Study in the Christian Tradition* (Evia, Greece: Denise Harvey, 1995), 62.

2. J. Stevenson, ed., *Creeds, Councils and Controversies: Documents Illustrative of the History of the Church A.D. 337–461* (London: SPCK, 1966), 115.

3. Vladimir Lossky, *The Mystical Theology of the Eastern Church* (Crestwood, NY: St. Vladimir's Seminary Press, 1997), 50.

Index

Phyllis Tickle is the founding editor of the Religion Department of *Publishers Weekly* and an authority on religion in America. A former academic and college dean, Tickle is the author of some two dozen books on the subject, including the bestselling volumes *The Great Emergence: How Christianity Is Changing and Why* and *Emergence Christianity: What It Is, Where It Is Going, and Why It Matters*. She makes her home with her physician husband on a small farm in rural West Tennessee.

Jon M. Sweeney is the editor in chief of Paraclete Press in Massachusetts, as well as an independent scholar, and author. Several of Jon's books have become History Book Club selections, and twice they have been featured on PBS's "Religion & Ethics Newsweekly." HBO has optioned his latest work of popular history, *The Pope Who Quit: A True Medieval Tale of Mystery, Death, and Salvation* (Image, 2012). He is also the recent editor and translator of *Francis of Assisi in His Own Words: The Essential Writings*, and co-authored a book about interfaith marriage with his wife, Rabbi Michal Woll, *Mixed Up Love: Relationships, Family, and Religious Identity in the 21st Century*.

Welcome to the story
that is still being told . . .

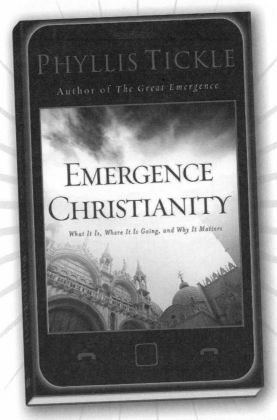

"You will find many wonderful things between the covers of this book: provocative questions and astute observations about sacred space, hierarchy, authority. Tickle's insights will help the church reflect on a larger question: How can we best serve the kingdom of God right now?"

— LAUREN F. WINNER, author of *Mudhouse Sabbath* and *Still: Notes on a Mid-Faith Crisis*

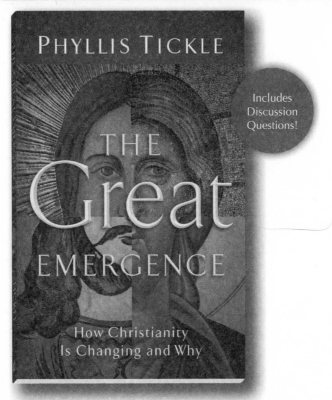